A Family At War

A Family At War

by

Emily Williams

The London Press

First published in Great Britain in 2004 by The London Press

British Library Cataloguing in Publication Data

Williams, Emily
A Family At War: a collection of First World War accounts
1. World War, 1914–1918 – Personal narratives
Title II. Bryant, Joti
940.4'81

ISBN: 0-9544636-4-1

Cover design by Mary Helen Fein

Page design and layout by Decent Typesetting – www.decenttypesetting.co.uk

Dedicated to and in memory of all the men who lost their lives during the Great War, and especially to those members of my family, past and present, who made this book possible.

Also to my dear family, to darling Alex and my wonderful friends Emma, Pauline, Wenna and Vafa.

Contents

Acknowledgements

My thanks is to all those who have helped me collect the various accounts:

- Rosemary and Harry St. John (my grandmother and uncle) for 'Tudor's Diary,' and Honorary Curator Captain (rtd.) P. D. Marr of the Fusiliers Museum of Northumberland at Alnwick Castle for permission to use it.
- Mike Williams for lending me Alfred Williams' letters.
- Julian Williams for J F Williams' diary.
- Patricia and Jane Wilson for providing the letters from H M Wilson.
- John Robins for lending the collection of C Carver's letters, and the Carver family for allowing me to use them.
- Colonel G and James Williams, for Stephen Williams' 1st World War notes.
- Michael St. John for extracts taken from his autobiography, A Tale of Two Rivers.
- Hugh and Alice Williams for their love and support.

Thanks also to my editor Joti Bryant, to Mary Helen Fein for designing the front cover, and to the publishers, The London Press. For permission to quote from The Trench, I would like to thank Richard van Emden and the Bantam Press. I have tried to make contact with both the publishers of 'Canon's Folly' and the writer of the web site *www.greatwar.com* (which provided much of the day to day information) but without success.

I have made every reasonable effort to acknowledge the ownership of the copyrighted material included in this volume. Any errors that may have occurred are inadvertent, and this will be corrected in subsequent editions provided notification is sent to the authors. Finally, special thanks to Harry St. John for suggesting that I research Tudor's diary in the first place.

Prologue and Introduction

I was born in Devon in 1979, educated at home before taking my A Levels at Tavistock College. I then went to Exeter University to read mathematics and teacher training. My interest in the 1st World War began a few months after I graduated when I visited the battlefields in Northern France. With the aid of my great grandfather's World War I diary, I found the field south of Ypres near Wytschaete, in which he was wounded. The same day I also visited the grave of my great uncle, in Vermelles.

In the months that followed I researched the lives of these two men and began to piece together theirs and other war stories to form my family's history of the 1st World War.

The nine people whose stories now make up this book are either related to me or were friends of the family. Their verbatim accounts take various forms; diaries, letters and memoirs. I have also added a chronology of the events of the 1914–1918 War.

The accounts start in late June 1914.

Tudor St John (aged 34)

In 1914 he was adjutant of the 4th Battalion of the Northumberland

Fusiliers based at Portsmouth and married to Madge with two sons,

Roger my grandfather, and Michael.

My Great Grandfather.

Alfred Williams (aged 17)

(also known as Didden)

In 1914 he was a cadet on HMS Cumberland about to take his final exams.

My paternal Grandfather.

John Williams (aged 23)

(also known as J F Williams)

In 1914 he was serving on HMS Russell and brother to Robert and Alfred Williams.

My Great Uncle.

Robert Williams (aged 26)

He was the older brother of John and Alfred.

A heart defect had prevented him from joining the army but on the declaration of war he enlisted. He eventually joined the Grenadier Guards as a machine gunner.

My Great Uncle.

Christian Carver (aged 17)

(also known as Crick and C C Carver)

In 1914 he was nearing the end of his studies at

Rugby School. Nephew of W H Carver

and cousin of my father's mother.

Major William Carver (aged 46)

(also known as W H Carver)

In 1914 he had recently been re-commissioned into the Army after serving 17 years in the Militia.

My Great Grandfather.

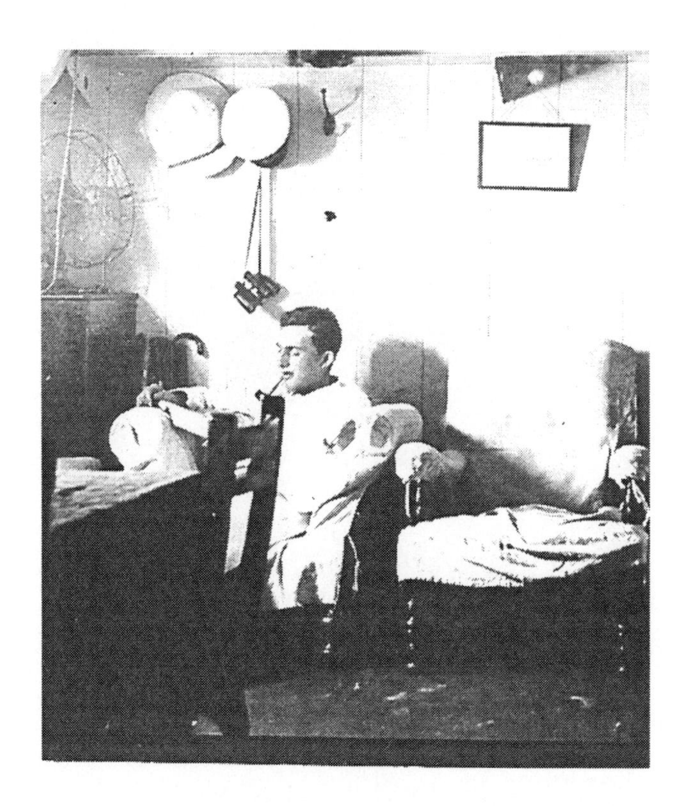

Hubert Wilson (aged 17)

(also known as H M Wilson)

In 1914 he was also a cadet on HMS Cumberland and

became a lifelong friend of Alfred Williams.

He eventually became my Great Uncle when he

married W H Carver's older daughter Patricia,

mentioned as Peggy in his letters.

Canon Martin Andrews

In 1914 he was working in Australia when war broke out and enlisted shortly after.

He became a good friend of Alfred Williams and

officiated at my parents marriage.

Stephen Williams

In 1914 he was a cadet at the Royal Military Academy, Sandhurst.

Cousin to Alfred Williams.

Family Tree

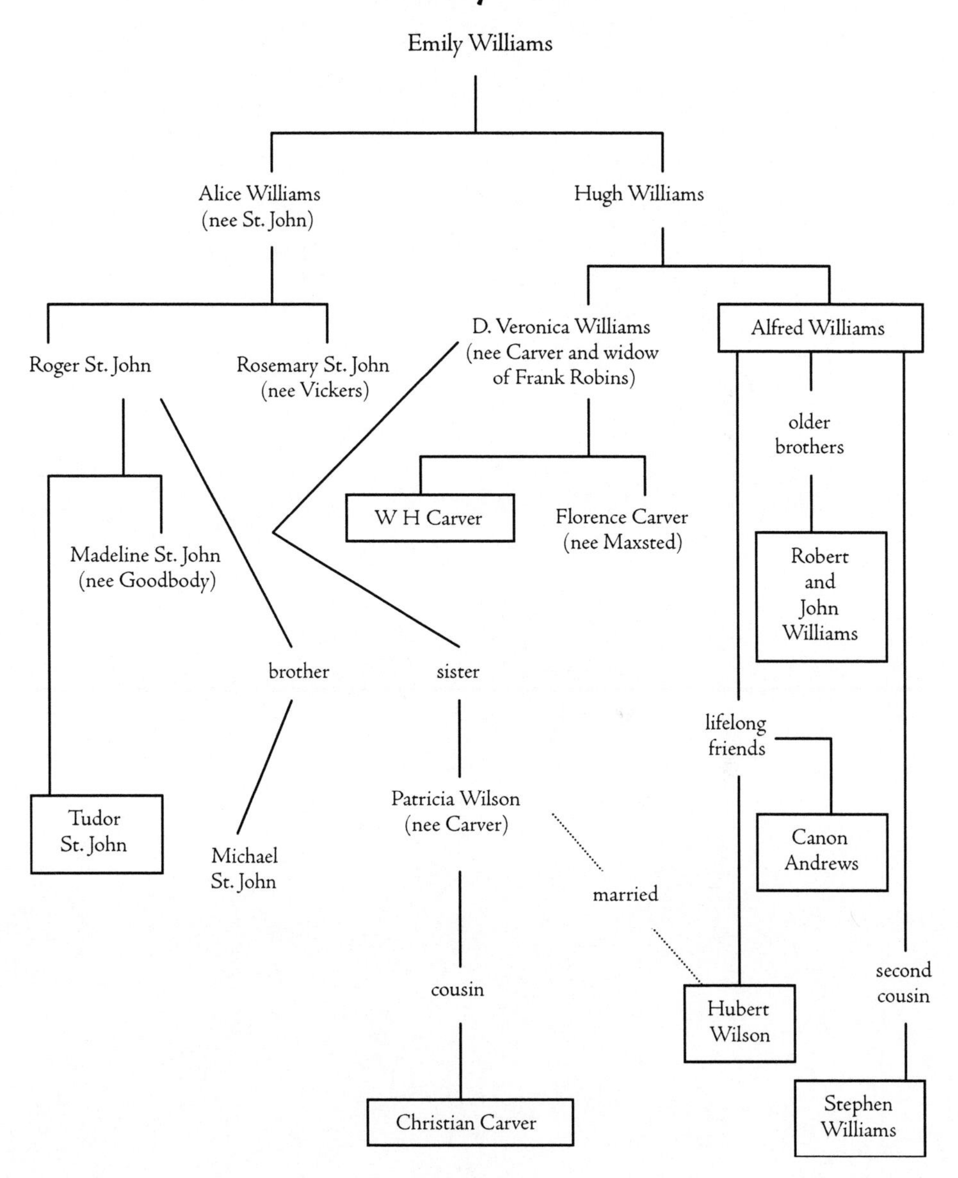

Emily Williams
Alice Williams
(nee St. John)
Hugh Williams
Roger St. John
Rosemary St. John
(nee Vickers)
D. Veronica Williams
(nee Carver and widow
of Frank Robins)
Alfred Williams
older
brothers
W H Carver
Florence Carver
(nee Maxsted)
Madeline St. John
(nee Goodbody)
Robert
and
John
Williams
brother
sister
lifelong
friends
Patricia Wilson
(nee Carver)
Tudor
St. John
Michael
St. John
Canon
Andrews
married
cousin
Hubert
Wilson
second
cousin
Christian Carver
Stephen
Williams

Places mentioned in the text

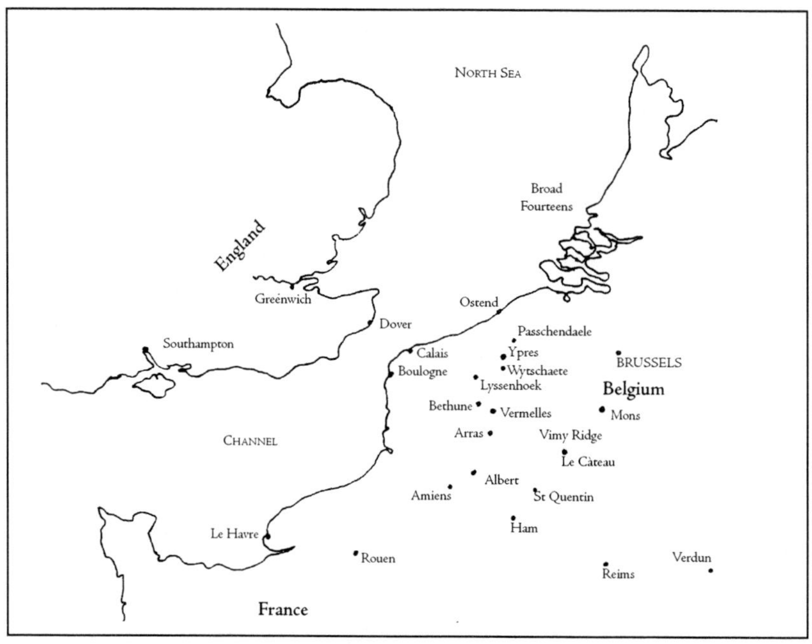

1914

28th June 1914

Sarajevo Assassination.

Alfred Williams

My one big fear was that the war would start before I got to sea. I thought, if war started before I got to sea, how in hell could I ever catch up with the older chaps, who were already seagoing cadets, who might gain awards and medals for bravery in action?

This may now sound far-fetched but at the time it was really true. Once I was a seagoing cadet, I had travelled round Tattenham corner, and was finally in sight of the winning post, which was war. On the 'Cumberland' I spent June 1914 doing Seamanship and in the monthly term order I came 18th. This was a tremendous moment in my life.

July 1914

Austria declared it would take strong measures against Serbia. Britain anounced that it would follow the same policy of mediation as in 1912.

Tudor St John

I can well remember the day that the idea of the probability of a European war came into my mind. It was on the day that the contents of Austria's note to Serbia were made public in the English press, and like many others I wondered what was behind that historic document.

I remember that friends had motored over from Hamble on that day and the conversation turned somewhat light-heartedly on the presumptuous tone of the note. I remember saying something to the effect that I wasn't at all sure it was a subject for light-hearted treatment; which lead them to ask, 'Do you think England will really go to war with Germany?'

This question non-plussed me in a way, for although I thought and said that if Austria persisted in her threat and Serbia didn't knuckle under to her, an Austro Serbian war was inevitable. This would drag in Russia and Germany, then France, and then England was bound to come in.

Yet the idea of this Armageddon was unthinkable. That it was so unthinkable is no wonder to me when I consider that for years the Government had made out that such a war was impossible.

Outspoken patriots were no more than terrified fanatics or feeble-minded dotards clinging tenaciously to a spot in the limelight of public affairs, in which they had basked – however honourably – for too long a period. I can still clearly remember friends saying to me at parting, 'If you do have to go and fight, mind you kill heaps of Germans, they are a vile lot of people.'

From this date until the day that saw us actually on the sea en route for France, events of great magnitude crowded one upon the other in such rapid succession that I find I have but a very confused impression of all that did happen. I remember a short period of very high tension and expectancy until Austria refused to accept Serbia's reply. Russia began to mobilise its troops.

Then came a further period of nervous apprehension as to what our government would do, followed by a curiously mixed feeling of relief and despondency when at last the 'Precautionary Period' was ordered: relief at the thought that the nation was not going to evade its obligations, and despondency at the thought of what this war was to be like.

I never had any illusions as to the war being a picnic, though I likewise had no idea as to the degree of 'frightfulness' to which Germany would go. From this confusion of recollection one or two events stand out more or less vividly in my mind's eye. First of these was the reception of the order proclaiming the 'Precautionary Period'.

27th July

Germany rejects Grey's proposal of a Four-Power Conference.

29th July

Cabinet rejects Grey's proposal to support France. After the meeting Asquith supports Churchill's decision to prepare a fleet. Government departments ordered to implement precautionary measures.

Tudor St John

I had been playing lawn tennis that afternoon at the United Services Club and at teatime there were rumours of the arrival of the order. There had been one or two similar rumours previously, and at first I was inclined to be sceptical about this one, but I noticed the arrival of several orderlies that synchronised with the hurried departure of most of the officers, so about 5.30pm I started off on my bicycle to barracks, to find out what was going on.

I was met on arrival with the news that the Battalion was to parade at 6.00pm in marching order. I dashed off to my house, which was about one and a half miles from barracks, got into my uniform as quickly as possible and dashed back to parade.

According to the scheme for Precautionary Measures, I was not detailed for any specific duty. But owing to so many officers being away on courses of instruction and on leave etc., I found that I had to depart at 7.30pm and proceed to Bedhampton, by train, and guard the waterworks at that spot.

I sent Saunders, my servant, with a hurried note to Madge, my wife, and orders to collect some bedding and food for me and to come on to Bedhampton by the next possible train.

We got to Bedhampton somewhere about 8.00pm that night. I forget whether my command consisted of 25 or 50 men; anyway it was entirely inadequate for the duty imposed upon it. This was a fine and typical example of the way we do this sort of thing in dear old England.

Apparently what had happened was this. Some bright, highly placed official, being struck with the idea that a war with Germany was possible (if not probable, in spite of government assurances to the contrary), conceived the still more brilliant idea that much damage to vulnerable points could be done by Secret Service Agents, immediately after the outbreak of war. 'Very clever idea,' said the members of the Army Council, (or whatever the body of officials who dealt with 'bright ideas'), 'we will decide what strategic points shall constitute a 'vulnerable point' and instruct local commanders in chief to draw up a scheme for their defence and protection.'

With regard to the Bedhampton Water Works, I can imagine either of two things occurring on receipt of this order by the C.I.C. First, a sensible well-paid and conscientious Staff Officer was sent out to investigate. He reports that either a large body or adequate protective works would be required.

Possibly his report is forwarded and recommended, or perhaps the C.I.C. has his own instructions with regard to cost. At any rate the 'adequate protective works' idea is firmly squashed owing to its entailing an expenditure of money, and the large body of men needed was impracticable owing to the multitudinous calls upon the local personnel during the Precautionary Period.

Secondly, and this course may have been pursued on the breakdown of the first, a regimental tour was organised with the idea of evolving answers to this and one or two similar problems. A team was created – of more or less fed-up, underpaid officers – to evolve hypothetical solutions; based upon the material to hand, working under the impression that by so doing they were practising the art of making war as it should be made.

At all events, whichever or whatever method was employed I found myself at Bedhampton with an inadequate force and a few sheets of typed orders and instructions. These were of a certain amount of assistance in enabling me to see clearly for myself how impossible it was to prevent a determined man from destroying the waterworks should he so desire.

I set to work at once to do what I could by getting hold of the manager and posting sentries as far as possible on the most exposed and vulnerable spots: such as valves, exposed piping, power houses, etc.

I also, with some difficulty, made it clear that I had not brought the men there merely as an illustration of 'life in the Army', or for their edification.

I organised a system of passes signed by the manager and countersigned by myself for the use of men actually necessary to the works.

I then rang up Headquarters and reported my arrival and told them what I thought of it all, and then tried to get the RE people to get me some materials for defensive purposes. It took me 24 hours, (or it may have been longer), to get through to the RE owing as I learned afterwards, to the absence of the entire staff. They were all at the Goodwood Races!!!

H M Wilson
H M S Cumberland

Dear Mother,

You can't imagine the confusion here. We got a wireless message at Cowes about 7pm last night, recalling everyone from leave and another one later ordering us to prepare to mobilise.

We left Cowes this morning and are on our way to Devonport now. We have all been told off to ships and shall probably go to them shortly – perhaps today if they mobilise. I am going to the 'Euryalus', a big cruiser (bigger than this) and 12 of us are staying here.

The rest have been told off. I will try and send you a wire as soon as we know anything or if we get on these ships. I never thought it would come to this. Last night we cleaned the guns and connected up the telephones and sights. There was tremendous confusion. We ought to have coaled up today at Portsmouth but they will do so at Devonport. We shall probably go to the Royal Naval barracks till we get appointed.

Your loving son,

Hubert

31st July

London informed that Russia and Austria have ordered general mobilisation. Germany proposes to mobilise unless Russia stops all military measures within 12 hours and demands to know whether France will remain neutral. Grey asks France and Germany whether they intend to respect Belgian neutrality. France says 'yes', but Germany refuses to reply. British Cabinet still not prepared to give France a definite pledge of assistance.

H M Wilson

TELEGRAM
TO WILSON, HEDDON'S GATE, PARRACOMBE.

'LANDED AT KEYHAM COLLEGE. IN CASE OF MOBILISATION SHALL GO TO EURYALUS, CHATHAM. KING.'

Royal Naval College
Keyham, Devonport

Dear Mother,

I hope you got my wire. We came up here this morning in case we have to mobilise, which depends upon whether Russia and Germany go to war. If we have to mobilise I shall go to the Euryalus at Hull. Don't say too much about this as they have threatened to stop all mail in and out of Portsmouth if too much gets into the papers. We belong to the 3rd Battle Fleet and are used as decoys. We left Cowes in the middle of the night last Wednesday in a great hurry and came to Plymouth. I believe the Cumberland has left for the South Atlantic but I am not sure. Don't get anxious,

Your loving son,

Hubert

H M Wilson

Dear Mother,

We are just leaving Devonport for Chatham. We leave here at seven, get to London at 3.00am and then onto Chatham at 8am I have sent various wires but I don't suppose they will turn up. I am going to the Euryalus. We have been in high fever packing chests, etc. I expect we will have a fine journey tonight. Don't be anxious. I must stop now.

Your loving son,

Hubert

1st August

King George V calls for Russia's restraint. Russia does not reply to German ultimatum. French mobilisation ordered at 3.40pm Germany orders general mobilisation at 5.00pm and declares war on Russia at 7.10pm

⊸ 2nd August ⟜

German troops enter Luxembourg. Cabinet advises Britain to intervene if Germany attacks French fleet. Germany advises Belgium that it will invade France (to repulse a French attack), and demands that France co-operate.

H M Wilson
Grosvenor Hotel
London, W5

Dear Mother,

I expect you have gathered by now that I am on the Euryalus. I think she will be commencing destroying. If this war lasts any time we shan't go back to the Cumberland. I don't suppose there will be much chance of writing as we will probably be at sea for some time. Write to the Euryalus c/o G. P. O. not Special Service.

Your loving son,

Hubert

⊸ 3rd August ⟜

Belgium refuses Germany's ultimatum. Cabinet approves mobilisation of both fleet and army. Germany declares war on France. King of Belgium appeals to King George for diplomatic intervention. Orders given for British mobilisation.

J F Williams

Still preparing for war. At 8.00pm a signal was given that hostilities would begin at midnight. Feeling of relief that we had not backed out of it.

4th August

German troops enter Belgium. Grey sends Germany ultimatum to withdraw by midnight. When ultimatum expires British cabinet agrees to send BEF to France. War declared on Germany. Mobilisation orders issued. Germany declares war on Belgium. Germans attack city of Liege.

J F Williams

Rumours of battles but nothing confirmed. Three of our fleet has left to join the first fleet. It is hard to imagine that we are at war lying here in this enclosed harbour. Let us hope we get out of it soon as it has a bad effect on everyone. Coaled ship but only a very little.

Alfred Williams

In July I did a month of Heat and Steam. To me 'Heat and Steam' was the most difficult of all subjects and in this subject I came out almost bottom. We sat our exam in the H.M.S. Cumberland only for the war alert to arrive in the middle and we all went into Devonport Barracks, and the Cumberland went to her war station.

But the 'Heat and Steam' exam followed us, and once again we sat down to it, and once again the alert came. This time it was for good and my feelings towards this event were, 'Thank God the War has started and therefore put an end to Heat and Steam!' We took our sea chests from Devonport across London, humping them ourselves, and arrived at Chatham dockyard to be told that no wood was to be taken onboard. We were just allowed to take what we could fit into a kit bag and suitcases, and left the sea chests to be stored in Chatham. I never saw mine again.

H M Wilson
HMS Euryalus
Chatham

Dear Mother,

I hope you have got my letters and wires. We got onboard on Sunday afternoon. I have never had such a Sunday in my life. Everyone working three times as hard as ordinary. We have got a lot of work and I have been taking my 6" guns crew most of this morning. They are fairly smart, as they are Marines.

Most of the crew are reservists. We have got a very nice lot of officers but this ship is frightfully slack compared with the Cumberland. I was on watch from 4 to 8 this morning.

Our job is greatly to prevent panic. They serve us out with a revolver or hypodermic syringe to squirt the wounded if they make too much noise and go mad. The surgeon fellow showed us some rudiments of first aid. There is hardly a chair or door in the place; all the wood on boats is sent ashore.

So far we are not getting any pay which is scandalous. I think we are going out tonight to be in readiness. In action the men have brass tallies stitched on in case they get blown up. When I saw them doing manoeuvres last week I never thought we should have the real thing so soon.

We have been getting up ammunition etc., and coal and ash sacks are piled around the engines. The only worry is how the reserves will shape up. I think they are useless. They haven't any discipline. That is where the Yeomanry will fail.

We have had orders for a long time to sink any Germans we see, and the gun crews are at their guns all night in case of any zeppelins trying to blow up the oil tanks or docks. Don't be anxious. Must stop now as gun crew is going to loading practise.

Your loving son,

Hubert

Alfred Williams

We were now sea-going cadets. We went up the gangway onto the quarterdeck of the Euryalus, to be met by an elderly Lieutenant Commander Cole-Hamilton, who was, I suppose, about 35, and he had a beard. He was Officer of the Watch, and was twiddling his signet ring. (What absurd trivialities remain in the memory!).

'Good Lord,' he says, 'What have you come for?' At this moment an angel appeared in the form of the Chief Yeoman of Signals, and he handed to the Officer of the Watch a signal announcing our pending arrival, so all was well. Down we went into the gunroom.

The order of the day was,'All surplus wood was to be put ashore to reduce the risk of fires.' So all lavatory doors were replaced by canvas, and the tables, chairs and settees of the gunroom were put ashore. Only one soapbox remained in it.

We were all shunted into the wardroom. After a short time the Wardroom Officer came to the conclusion that whatever the added risk of fire might be, some things were worse than death, and to have eight 17 and a half year old boys in the wardroom was one of these things. So back we went to the refurbished gunroom.

Tudor St John

The next event, which is still clear to me, was the arrival of the order to mobilise. We had been expecting it hourly ever since I returned from Bedhampton on the previous Friday. During this interval of expectancy men had been confined to barracks and officers were only allowed out for two hours at a time. I slept on my camp bed in Dick Mitchell's room. There was very little really in the shape of work to be done.

We did all we could but soon reached a point where we were stopped by not having the official order to mobilise. Dick Gatehouse, whose wife was staying with us, and I used to go home for breakfast, spend the morning in Barracks, and then used to spend two hours at home and return to sign our names in the guard book and go back for another two hours. It was during one of these returns to barracks on the Tuesday that the long desired order to mobilise arrived. I remember I was standing talking to Colonel Ainslie and one or two others when the telegraph boy gave the Colonel a message. He simply opened it and read the one word 'mobilise,' on which we all quickly vanished and began the series of carefully planned 'jobs' which were required to be done in order to bring the battalion from a peace footing to a war footing in both men and material.

J F Williams
HMS Lord Nelson

(To be forwarded on my death to my father.)

Dear Father,

I am leaving you what I have. Will you do what you think fit with it? I should like Alfred to benefit by it if he lives through the war all right.

Your loving son,

John F Williams

Robert Williams

Having originally intended to join the Army (an injury to his heart had prevented him from doing so), Robert Williams immediately offers his services in any capacity in which he could be of use. As a result he is appointed chauffeur to General Woodhouse. He took his own car to France and was thus occupied through the winter of 1914/15.

5th August

Austria–Hungary declares war on Russia. Great Britain mobilises.

J F Williams

Still preparing for war. We leave this evening but there will be no big naval action until the German High Sea Fleet is forced to sea by public opinion or lack of food and stores. Censorship has begun as of this evening.

6th August – 24th August

Battle of the Frontiers commences.

J F Williams

Official report of the sinking of a German mine layer. We hear that Kitchener has gone to the War Office. Will this mean that the Expeditionary Force will be sent across into Belgium to assist them? Many rumours of captured merchantmen.

7th August

Kitchener makes public appeal for volunteers. (By the end of the year a million men will have joined up.) British Expeditionary Force begin landing in France. Germans penetrate Liege.

J F Williams

Routine battle exercise during the afternoon. Wish we could have more of these as they do a lot of good. We may be required to cover the Expeditionary Force as they cross the Channel.

Tudor St John

It was calculated that we should require five days to complete the work, and we did it in that time without any hitch, and on the following Sunday (9th Aug) we were again waiting – this time for the order to embark.

H M Wilson

Dear Mother,

I hope I shall hear from you soon, I haven't heard anything since leaving the Cumberland. This has to be read before it goes, as they are very particular about censoring. We aren't allowed to put in the date or anything like that. Where is Father quartered? Have any men about the place volunteered? I suppose the horses have gone as remounts.

The Germans seem to have got it pretty hot at Liege. I can't quite imagine what the state of affairs can be like at home. Did they let you know I was coming here? I will write as often as possible but of course we are at sea nearly all of the time except for coaling. I hope we get some leave when this is over. I don't think it will be this side of Christmas.

Your loving son,

Hubert.

8th August

J F Williams

Coaled in the morning after orders to steam by 11.45. Destination unknown. Imagine it's to do with the Expeditionary Force. Cleared away, trained and loaded all guns and then proceeded up the channel keeping well out to sea. We have no minesweepers with us. We have been informed that we are shadowing the crossing of the expeditionary force and that this will probably meet with some attention on the part of the Germans. We all have our ideas as to what our part may be should the High Fleet make a dash through the Straits of Dover and down the Channel. Let us hope that the Grand Fleet will not be far behind them. The length of time, for which we would be able to hold them would I think, be short unless we can get some minelayers to help us.

9th August

French cavalry enter Belgium. Belgians fall back to the Dyle. Germany's offers of peace to Belgium are rejected.

J F Williams

We hear the Expeditionary Force is to start today. A much fuller day. The ship is very hot.

Tudor St John

We employed this period of enforced idleness in getting the thousand odd men who now made up the Battalion, as far as possible fit to march. Most of the reservists who rejoined the colours were soft and we were fully occupied in hardening them, getting them used to their equipment, the pattern of which was new to most of them.

We taught them as much as possible a few of the principles of scientific warfare which we had spent so much time and trouble to teach to the few men who were with the colours at that moment. Here again plenty of proof was accorded me of the truth of one of my pet theories, which was that our Army in peacetime was too highly trained. We had taught the peace men a great deal and had shown them how to act for themselves and mix with their comrades. But when war actually occurred they were intermingled as a small minority in a battalion composed for the great part of reservists who had been trained in a different school, and who had forgotten most, if not all, of that which they had been taught.

The result was that the highly trained man found that he was unable to carry out the systems of movement and combination which he had been taught were so imperative to success because his reservist comrades didn't understand what he meant.

9th August – 16th August

British Expeditionary Forces continue to land in France. France declares war on Austria-Hungary.

12th August

J F Williams

Heard of size and rough outline of Expeditionary Force. Four transports have been seen going over. We will steam on our patrol the same as before. Much discussion as to whether the High Sea Fleet will break through the Straits of Dover and if so whether by night or day. My money is on the former. At present they are not sure where the fleet is. I think Norway, as they will be independent there to act when they think fit. The heat in the ship is still great.

Tudor St John

On Wednesday evening we got our embarkation orders. These arrived at 7.00pm and were orders to entrain on the following morning at 9.00am I don't propose to dwell on the pains of parting. I dislike saying goodbye to people I like at any time so I found the wrench of parting from my family a very severe business. I never said goodbye to Roger at all. I left the house at 6.00am and bade farewell to Madge and my mother in barracks just before we marched out.

13th August

J F Williams

The heat still blunders on. Our work is important and yet we are sent to sea on an almost fixed patrol with only one light cruiser and no means of searching, watching or taking into harbour any of the Swedish sailing vessels and tugs etc which always seems to be hanging around the fleet.

We started sending the ships to Portsmouth to coal before taking more men across. Only a short period of time is allowed for this. I believe this is one of the first big days as far as numbers of men are concerned for the BEF to get over. We have declared war on Austria.

This bad ink is due to the pen being topped up for the third time with water. A suspicious vessel came near our lines about 6.30 tonight. Later on we intercepted a signal to patrol flotilla warning them to look out for a vessel of a certain description flying a Dutch ensign and carrying a German admiral on board. It seems to be the same one we saw though by the time the signal was received it was too dark to look for her.

It makes me so annoyed to think that here we are steaming up and down doing our job but have no orders to search and deal with such vessels. I feel we are being made into bait. It may also mean that much of our work becomes useless. The presence of many sailing craft continues.

H M Wilson

Dear Mother,

Thank you for all the letters and books. There are 8 of us here from the Cumberland. We saw some of the Expeditionary Force going across today. My chest is at Royal Naval Barracks, Chatham. There are a lot of towels and pillowcases in it. My trunk and bag are at Keyham. I don't suppose I shall ever see them again. We get a press telegram nearly every morning, which gives us some idea of what is going on. The only thing I expect is the English government will be too generous and not let the Germans be exterminated.

Your loving son,

Hubert

Tudor St John

We waited for over an hour at Portsmouth Station before our train departed and ran through to Southampton when we embarked upon the S.S. Norman of the Union Castle Line. The 1st half of the battalion finished embarking by about midday, and we got the entire battalion on board by 3.00pm including the mess hampers – for which we were thankful as we were getting quite hungry after a very early breakfast.

There was a small doubt for a time as to whether or not the ship would sail at all as the seamen appeared to think that their country's pressing need for a rapid movement of the Expeditionary Force to France was a propitious and heaven sent moment for them to go on strike for exorbitant wages.

Fortunately the wiser councils of their leaders prevailed and at about 5.00pm on 13th of August we cast off from the jetty and steamed away for the Solent, en route as we found out after, for Le Havre.

Soon after sailing we were given messages from the King and Lord Kitchener, which we read to the troops. Of course it soon got dark after we left England, and being pretty well tired out with worry and emotion I turned into the cabin which my early arrival and natural acquisitiveness had secured me for my sole and exclusive benefit. I woke up at midnight under the impression that we were there, but we were by no means at our journey's end.

We steamed slowly along through endless docks and narrow channels in which one could have jumped from the ship onto the quay on the other side with the greatest of ease. After a couple of hours of this sort of progress I got fed up with it and turned in again and slept soundly for an hour or more when I was again awakened and informed that the ship was berthed and we were about to disembark. I hurried up on deck and found we were tied up outside a shed.

14th August

Sir John French lands at Boulogne.

J F Williams

We proceeded to Dover to coal at 6.00am and were finished by 3.00am We managed to get a few papers and saw an aeroplane flying overhead. Also some fresh food which was much needed. Dover was full of minelayers and destroyers. Total absence in the papers of naval news and also no mention of the BEF. We proceeded from Dover at three o'clock and heard that most of the infantry was already across.

A submarine patrol is to be started at the mouth of the German North Sea harbours. The price of food ashore didn't appear to have gone up much. We re-joined the fleet at about four o'clock and the Admiral came aboard again. Our mail was brought out from Portsmouth, which was very much appreciated. Shortly after leaving Dover we saw the Sentinel going across with the Commander in Chief, Sir John French, on board.

Tudor St John

At about 4.00am we disembarked and formed up inside the shed, which by its smell appeared to be the summer residence of a couple of tonnes of putrefied meat and fish. We sat here for two hours during which time some of us got some coffee.

Shortly after 6.00am we proceeded to our rest camp led there by two diminutive French boy scouts. The road to the rest camp lay for the first few miles through the slums of Le Havre. It was rather early for demonstrations by the natives, but there was evidence of great welcoming to those who had arrived before we did. Bunting was plentiful everywhere, and of the few natives we did see many of them bore evidence of frequent libations to the glory of the allies.

After an hours' march, the sun which had been shielded behind mist, began to make its presence felt. The route began to climb up a rather trying hill and the road became sandy and badly metalled. At first a man here and there sat down by the roadside but soon they fell out like flies.

We tried every means to urge them on, but soft words and harsh and even hard actions failed to move them. The truth was that they were done. Being soft and not having any breakfast are not good as a combination on which to perform a trying march. We eventually reached our camp, and with one or two exceptions who were taken to hospital, all the men turned up fairly soon after we arrived.

Our camp, which was supposed to accommodate 4,000 troops, was pitched on a high stubble field. There was no shade and the sun was very powerful. We lay about for several hours waiting for the arrival of our transport with food, but none came. At about 3.00pm having had nothing in the shape of meat or drink except water since the previous evening, I boiled some water and made soup with oxo cubes. This helped a little but by seven o'clock I was ravenous. We had tried the farm nearby to see if anything could be got from there but they were cleaned out.

At about 7.00pm I went down the hill to the village and got what to me tasted better than any meal I have eaten – a large omelette and some cold ham, with a bottle of red wine, at a little wayside cafe. We got back to camp at 9.00pm and an hour later some of our transport rolled up and I got my valise and turned in.

15th August

J F Williams

Very wet watch, heavy rain. I think we saw the cavalry crossing today. A large transport passed down between the lines today and cheers were freely exchanged. Lucky fellows. They will probably see and do far more than we shall. But I suppose we must hope for the best. The Grand Fleet is reported to be some fifty miles north of the Thames estuary.

Tudor St John

Somewhere near midnight there came a terrific thunderstorm that woke us all up. It rained in torrents and made the stubble ground most unpleasant to lie upon, besides the noise of the rain on the canvas preventing us from sleeping. The rain continued in a somewhat subdued form all Saturday and the field became a regular bog with each furrow like a miniature lake. It was a most unpleasant day.

We managed to cook some food but eating was no joy with everything soaked. Walking was not walking but wading in liquid mud and we were all wet through. We got orders to move at midnight and had the devil's own job to get the transport out of the field.

16th August

First B.E.F. contingent completes landing.

Tudor St John

The march down to Le Havre took us four hours with constant halts to deal with jibbing horses, but we reached the railway station at last and made much quicker work of putting the horses and wagons on the train. We then found a café which opened for us, and we got some much appreciated coffee at about 6.00am and went to our seats in quite comfortable 1st class carriages where we soon fell asleep through sheer weariness. At about 7.30 am I half woke up and found we had begun to move but I was soon asleep again and didn't really wake up till near 10.00am when we found we were dawdling through some peaceful part of the French countryside. We didn't know where we were or what was our destination and neither did the guard or the engine driver; at least that's what they said. At lunchtime or thereabouts, we got to Rouen where we fed the men and ourselves and changed the engine. The new driver seemed to think we were going to Amiens and his supposition turned out to be correct as we reached Amiens at about 5.00pm.

From Rouen to our destination our journey was a triumphal procession. At each little village and at each level crossing even, there were wildly cheering crowds who cried, 'Vive les Anglais,' with gusto and urged us with much pantomime gesture to 'Coupe' the German 'Gorges.' At Amiens we again changed engines and learnt that we were going 'north' but it was not until we actually reached it that we found out that our destination was a place called Landrecies. We detrained at about 10.30pm and marched to our billets, the men in a very flea-ridden odoriferous barracks and the officers in a nice clean girls' school where we revelled in beds with real sheets. The rightful owners had departed and the school was being got ready for use as a hospital or dressing station.

17th August

Renewed French advance. Sir John French establishes headquarters at Le Chateau.

Tudor St John

We got turned in at about 1.00am and I was early astir next morning. After a rather indifferent breakfast in a cabaret I went up to barracks and was told I was to go on a bicycle to a place called Noyelles to take over billets there. Accompanied by the cyclist section I got myself, we proceeded on our journey, which was fortunately only 10 kilometres long. I got to the village of Noyelles without mishap and proceeded to find billets for the regiment. This was no easy job as I am not a good linguist and had not been given an interpreter but I managed it just in time before the Battalion got there.

17th August – 21st August

Kaiser orders destruction of General French's 'contemptible little army'.

J F Williams

Have been ordered to proceed to Portsmouth for dry-docking and bottom scraping on account of big coal consumption. We arrived at 3.30pm and were taken into the harbours to dry dock C. Got a good nights sleep in cabin while the dock was pumped. The following day we got provisions on board and flooding started about 7pm. Leave was up at 11pm.

Tudor St John

We stayed at Noyelles from Monday August 17th till Friday 21st during which time, except for the foreign language and the unusual comfort of billets, we might have been doing easy manoeuvres at home. The weather was glorious and as we got no newspapers we had very little to remind us of the war.

We passed the days in mild Company training or route marching while bathing in a deep and sluggish stream in the afternoon. This same stream was the cause of our first causality – a death by drowning.

We had a few of the old fashioned sorts of orders too, one of them being no one was allowed to go outside his billeting area without a pass, and if he did go outside then he must be fully equipped and armed. This meant that to go to the only shop in the place, which was 200 yards outside our formal area, I had to don my warlike garb, though the officers and men in whose area the shop was situated visited it in shirtsleeves and slacks.

I remember an amusing incident in that shop. I was buying some soft shoes for my sore feet and there was a considerable crowd in the shop and a great hubbub. Presently I was appealed to for help. It appeared that some men wanted to buy some castor oil for their boots and no one knew the French for it.

The only aid was a French-English dictionary, but all references to 'huile' failed to get us out of the difficulty until I had the brilliant idea to demand of the M'mselle some 'huile pour le stomac du bebe.' At once came the reply 'Ah oui Monsieur, je comprends, c'est la Ricin'!! And what is more, the necessary oil was produced not from the shop but from a neighbour's nursery.

20th August

Brussels falls to Germans. Belgian army retreats to Antwerp.

J F Williams

Coaled early in the morning and took on ammunition. Very glad of our 48 hours off. I believe the German fleet is waiting for a fog and will then make one big rush across when concentration is impossible and try and land some troops. We hear two of their army corps are unaccounted for. Some say the Germans will not try and land and maybe they are right. The North Sea is big and our east coast is long but then our army is out of the country so it will be interesting to see what happens.

Tudor St John

On the Thursday evening we got our orders to pack up and move early on Friday. We packed up all right and at 7.00am we marched off, our destination being unknown.

21st August

British troops begin to move towards Mons.

J F Williams

Fewer transports crossing Channel now. Very little news.

Tudor St John

We marched for some miles to a place called La Longueville where we went into billets. Toppin and I were in a cottage with a bed each and the other boys dossed down on the floor. I was kept busy all day paying the company, and was not finished doing so when an orderly came to me at about 7.00pm to say that the C.O. wanted all captains at once.

I left the pay sheets to Sergeant Laws to settle up and finish, and went off to Headquarters where I found a collection of serious faces. As soon as we had all gathered the Colonel gave us a short lecture on the situation which he illustrated on a map by the aid of a solitary candle stuck in a bottle.

It appeared that the Germans had crossed the Belgium frontier and were marching west and we were to march at day break with the idea of meeting them and checking their advance and finally driving them back to Berlin and so home for Xmas!!

22nd August

Battle of Mons commences. French continue to fall back.

Tudor St John

We were ready to move off at 3.00am filled with suppressed excitement, which in my case was mixed with a certain amount of apprehension. However, both these feelings wore off as we swung along in the early morning haze of what turned out to be a brilliantly fine day. We crossed the battlefield of Malplaquet with its war memorial and were soon in Belgium.

Our route lay along the 'route pave' which we found very tiring to our already tired feet. Shortly after crossing the frontier we were halted while the field officers went to confer with the Brigadier. The result of the conference was that B and C Companies under Major Yatman moved to the head of the column and the march was resumed.

At the next halt we were told to proceed to and hold a portion of the railway and canal to the west of Mons. For the rest of the way our route lay through a series of mining villages in each of which we were greeted with enthusiasm, the inhabitants crowding about us and pressing on us gifts of eggs, chocolate, tobacco, fruit, matches, cigars etc.

I noticed that the signallers at the front got most of the swag, and so greedy were they that I should estimate each signaller got a dozen eggs and 2 lbs. of chocolate. At last I sent up to tell them to behave themselves and let some of the men behind get a chance, threatening with punishment the next signaller I caught taking anything even if it was pressed on to him.

About a mile from our objective we halted and threw out an advance guard of our own. B and C Companies were now out alone, and we proceeded more quietly. After going for half a mile we halted by our point and a long pause ensued, so I went on to see what was up and found the point was refreshing itself in a cabaret. I promised them a court martial and kicked them out and we went on. The court-martial did not come off as by the time we had a chance to hold it the men who were to be tried were missing and the N.C.O. was dead.

We reached the canal at Quaregnon at about midday and when I had been out and selected a spot for an advance post clear of the canal. I returned and made an inspection of the facilities and material for making as good a defence as was possible.

The canal was a double one. On the north or German side was the main waterway. On the south or allies' side was a narrower, deeper one used as a sort of flood aqueduct. In between these two waterways ran a broad bank about 100 feet wide on which ran the south towpath.

Just by the bridges this bank was rather wider and on the other side of the bridges were a couple of houses built up on the bank. The main waterway was bridged by a leaver bridge, which was raised to a perpendicular position by means of a hand winch to allow the passage of the barges.

The canal was approached from the allies' side by a rather irregularly built street, the houses on both sides going right up to the edge of the narrow canal. Only about 100 yards of this street directly commanded the bridge, at the end of which we had our supports behind a barricade. On the north side of the canal the ground was open for about 100 to 150 yards with the exception of the bridge keeper's house and garden which was just by the bridge on the east side. The winch that worked the bridge was unfortunately on the wrong side of the water for our purpose.

At the end of this clear space ran a railway parallel with the canal. Then came the open country, which was much intersected by deep dykes. In open space by the bridgehead was an enclosed yard, fenced with old rail sleepers. This we speedily demolished leaving the ground open.

As soon as possible we began to prepare the bridgehead for defence. Having demolished the sleeper built palisade we made an entanglement from the end of the houses on the north side to some level crossing gates. We built this with some barbed wire I requisitioned from an unwilling native and the wire fencing that guarded the railway line.

We jammed the gates of the level crossing and also erected an obstacle on the north edge of the bridge itself. Altogether it made it very unpleasant for anyone attempting to advance to the bridge by the main road or to deploy along either side of the main road into the open space. We left a small opening easily closable for the return of our advanced post that had orders to return as soon as a determined advance on the part of the Germans became evident.

I also notched and loopholed the walls of the bridgekeeper's house and his garden and arranged for a post of twelve men under Sergeant Panter to be here. The next defensive works were in the houses on the bank between the canals. One of these houses we demolished altogether as it screened the field of fire of the detachment we had entrenched in the gardens on the east side. The others we loopholed and barricaded.

The inhabitants of all houses near the bridge cleared out, bag and baggage. Some went gladly and others had to be coerced. One family we evicted three times from a house close to the bridge and each time they sneaked back to it by a back entrance. At the time I was terribly sorry for those poor people but in the light of after events I had come to the conclusion that many of them were of German sympathies. I am quite sure that the bridge keeper was a spy but though I suspected him at the time I had not time enough to watch him carefully.

The people I was most sorry for were the owners and inhabitants of five barges on the canal. At first I was contented to shift these barges from the north bank to the south bank but later on it seemed such a simple matter to get them back again across the canal that we decided to sink them. We got a RE Officer, who was preparing the bridge for demolition, to blow a hole in the bottom of each of them. The wretched owners had to depart in a hurry, taking with them such of their most treasured possessions as could be carried in a small bundle.

Their weeping and lamentations were loud and sorrowful, and men wept more bitterly than the women, who no doubt shared in a lesser, though quite appreciable degree with the children, the excitement of the prospective picnic-like existence they were so suddenly called upon to assume. The work of preparation kept us busy till darkness put a stop to it. We were much hindered by the crowds of curious sightseers who looked on with amazed delight at the unusual sight of strangely garbed soldiers destroying somebody else's property, and now and then I had to use strong measures to scatter them sufficiently to permit the men to work.

23rd August – 24th August

Battle of Mons sees B.E.F. briefly delay German advance. Japan declares war on Germany. Namur taken by the Germans.

J F Williams

This monotonous job of patrolling is finally at an end.

H M Wilson

Dear Mother,

Thank you for your letter. It's bad luck on Belgium but I don't think one need worry because the Germans are in Brussels. It really is extraordinary they weren't there six weeks ago. What a pity Japan has declared war. It is sure to mean trouble with us in the end.

Your loving son,

Hubert

Tudor St John

I slept that night on the floor of a butcher's and at daybreak we continued work of defensive preparation, making a strong barricade across the road at the bridge-head. We also loopholed every available wall and house.

I lost all sense and count of time, but it was well on in the day when the fighting began. We had heard many reports of the approach of the dreaded Bosche but had not seen anything of them ourselves.

The attack by the German artillery began first of all on two main bridges, one about a mile to the east of us, and the other about the same distance to the west.

On the previous evening our position had been well reconnoitred by a Taube aeroplane at which I had had a sporting shot and for so doing I got badly hauled over the coals by our 2nd in Command. He drew a blood-curdling picture of our position being given away and the lot of us massacred all owing to absurd lightness of heart.

As a matter of fact I stood on our bridge for quite an hour watching the fight going on at the other bridges. As we found out later on, the troops at both these bridges had a very bad time of it and were badly cut up.

The first sight of the enemy we got was seen by the detachment occupying the bridge-keeper's houses and garden, who saw the Germans advancing up the lane which came apparently from nowhere. They were advancing in fours and were not very far away so that much damage was done to them before the detachment retired to the barricade on the south side of the bridges.

Some of this detachment retired at once on sighting the enemy, which no doubt prevented loss to the enemy being more serious than it was. This would have been because fewer rifles were employed against them and the weakened detachment did not dare remain for long in so exposed a position – though Sergeant Panter remained for as long as he safely could and behaved all through with coolness and good sense.

His action certainly checked the German advance for a time and evidently sent them back for artillery for the next thing that happened was the arrival of high explosive shells on the bridge. A steady rain of shells, mostly high explosives, followed this.

One of the houses between the two bridges got badly treated. I thought the detachment inside it were done for and did not see any of them again for a fortnight when three of them turned up. They reported that they had stopped in the cellar of the house and watched the Germans pass along all that night and most of the following day.

The detachment to the west of these houses came in when the first shell arrived. My barrier across the road was getting rather crowded with the incoming detachments, who all seemed to desire to be near an officer and disliked the idea of going into any more houses. However I got some of them away into a prepared house in the rear of the barricade.

On the other hand one or two men on the barrier were convinced it was nicer to be inside a house, with all those nasty shells flying about in the open. The house on the right of the barrier was getting quite full when a high explosive crumped right into it doing it a lot of damage. The nervous ones came tumbling out of it again.

Under cover of this artillery fire the Germans had occupied the houses at the end of the main road, and when it stopped for a bit they sniped at us out of the windows making the barricade rather unpleasant, though most of their shots were going high. We were doing some damage too and any German who showed himself got a very warm reception.

Not many of them did show themselves and for a time there was quite a lull in the fighting though the periodical shell kept coming along. One of these burst on the road a yard or two in front of our barrier but except for being covered with dust and debris there was no harm done.

Early on in the proceedings one of my sergeants got very excited, shooting at some Germans on the canal bank. I could not see these from where I was and the man was very keen to point them out as they showed themselves.

After having knocked out four or five of them he called out to me, 'Can't you see them, Sir? There's another of the beggars over there quite plain in his red breeks and blue coat.' Bang! 'There 'e is, Sir, dead as mutton now.'

I never found out if they really were Frenchmen we had been shooting but I don't think they could possibly have been, and more likely were Germans in French uniform.

After an hour or so of this sort of game, (I lost count of time altogether) a new diversion was created. We were waiting ready for some Germans whom we had noticed trying to get round the corner of the street opposite to us when all of a sudden 3 or 4 little girls dashed out of a house.

They ran across the street to another house and then back again and then backwards and forwards once more. I called out to cease firing, which was done at once. The lull only lasted two or three minutes, during which time I could hear the children crying but it was long enough to enable the Germans to cut some of my barbed wire and to get round the coal sheds to the west.

At the time we couldn't believe it was anything more than a lucky coincidence for the Germans. But in the light of what we learned afterwards there can be no doubt it was a neatly arranged ruse for the carrying out of which they counted on (to them) our idiotic chivalry.

Anyway it was most successful from their point of view and the men who got to the coal shed made themselves very objectionable to the left flank of our barrier. One of their bullets hit my sword and tore away the scabbard so that I had to discard the weapon – to my great relief.

We had orders to retire as soon as there was any indication of the enemy getting round our flanks but it was impossible to say how things were going on either flank. Toppin and I held a council of war together, and as the flank bridges were very silent and the people in front of us were more and more active, we decided to try and get some definite information.

But at the same time the Germans opened fire on us at point blank range with a field gun they had brought down to within 400 yards of us. Fortunately they had a very bad field of fire but it was very unpleasant as they were firing shrapnel burst at the muzzle. We also got a report from Boyd, who was with a detachment on our left, that the Germans were massing men and some artillery in and near the coal sheds. He could not get a good view of them owing to the towpath in between the two canals being just too big to shoot over. We decided therefore to commence a retirement and I began to send men back in small driblets down a side street.

When most of the men had gone – in fact, only the Q.M.S. and myself were left – the R.E officer, and staff sergeant arrived to blow up our bridge. He reported to me that the Germans were over the bridges on both our flanks so things did not look too rosy. However he got to work on his job but found that the man who had laid the charge had only provided leads for the main canal and had not taken the second waterway into consideration.

Undaunted he went out in front of the barrier and got under the bridge near the canal, dragged himself through the water to the centre towpath and wriggled about there trying to find the leads to connect the charge. Unfortunately he could not find them and so he returned. It was a plucky action, particularly as he was wounded at the time. I reported the instance and was glad to see that the officer got the VC for it, although, poor chap, he was killed afterwards.

Meantime the Q.M.S. and I had been doing what was possible in the way of covering fire, and our barrier was getting most unhealthy, so as soon as he got back we cut and ran for it and luck being with us we got away without being hit.

I got round through gardens and back ways until I reached the railway line, along which I went until I joined the rest of the Company. Under the command of Major Yatman, we then began to retire, being joined by small detachments of different companies all the way.

This retirement was one of the most exhausting things I remember, so far as I was concerned. We had no time to waste and my job was to post covering parties. We had to defend every street corner until the column had turned the succeeding corner and the result was that by the time I had placed one post I had to run on and catch the column up and tell off and place the next. I would have given my kingdom for a horse and no mistake.

Luckily for us the Germans did not press their attentions onto us very closely and after doing a mile of streets in this way Yatman gave the order to close and push on with only a small moving rear guard to protect us.

A staff officer met us and told us where our rendezvous was and we said we could get to it quite easily across country. As we crested a small hill we saw about 800 yards in front of us quite a large body of Germans resting.

It was a great temptation to give them a few rounds of rapid fire, but they showed us we must be in a pretty nasty situation. So we came to the conclusion that, as providence had so far been kind to us in keeping the knowledge of our situation from the enemy, we had better continue in our endeavour. We turned about and after much weary marching we reached our rendezvous in Freameries by a circuitous route as dusk was falling, finding battalion Headquarters and two companies anxiously awaiting us.

We halted in a small street and sat down on the kerb where we halted after sending out one platoon to barricade and hold the Mons Road.

The retirement had made me hot and tired and, as I had not had any food since breakfast, I was also pretty hungry. But there was no food to be had, as we had no transport. However, I soon got cool and got a little sleep too lying in the gutter with my head on the kerb, but I woke up after half an hour's doze feeling very odd and stiff, and went into a cottage where I begged a chair and sat by the stove.

The cottagers were most kind although they were obviously afraid and knew that things were not going well. They provided me with coffee for which they refused payment, and were most interested in examining all my belongings and equipment. A photograph of Roger (my grandfather) delighted them beyond measure and all the family from Pere to Bebe were called in to kiss it. Not being much of a linguist I missed a lot of their ecstatic compliments. But Toppin translated some and being the old campaigner that he was, seemed to think that the production of the photo would be a good stunt to ensure the production of fresh vitals, etc. on future occasions.

At about 9.30pm all the officers were called out and we proceeded to a field about half a mile away where we were to dig ourselves in that night. On our way across the field to choose the site of our trenches, we suddenly came on a man lying prone in the grass.

He appeared to be drunk and our interpreter assured us that he was drunk, but both Toppin and I at the time thought that he was only acting drunk. We said so but it was considered to be a waste of precious time to take him back to headquarters, and so he was allowed to go free.

We sighted and marked out our trenches and by midnight had the company up and at work at the digging of them. The men were tired and it was a heartbreaking job to constantly have to almost kick them to work, which was to protect them from death.

During the night, on looking behind on one occasion, I noticed that in a row of houses some 500 yards away there was one house with an unblinded upper window with a lighted lamp in it. I again called Toppan's attention to this but we came to the conclusion that it was no good to take any action in the matter. At about an hour before daybreak we had got deep enough cover for our temporary needs and the men being deadbeat we sent out the usual patrols and stood quietly to arms.

24th August

British fall back from Mons.

J F Williams

News from Belgium is not looking good. Proceeded to Portsmouth for more scraping.

Tudor St John

As soon as it was beginning to grow light I went down to our right to locate exactly where the trenches were on the far side of some buildings and to try to find some means of fairly safe intercommunication. This took me about ten minutes and I had a few words with Dick Gatehouse, whose company were manning those trenches.

On the way back I stopped to light my pipe as it was now quite light, and to have a look around at the country generally. I had just got my pipe lit when a regular inferno of shellfire burst on us and around us.

I made rapid tracks for my trench and got safely into it. I have no doubt that our friend, the drunken man had been a spy and had given the enemy the line by means of the light in the house. All that morning the Germans shelled us with short intervals of quiet. During these respites I tried to get a look around as we had a bad field of fire, but it was no good and it was most unpleasant as someone was sniping me from behind all the time.

After two or three hours of this game, Gatehouse walked around to see and said that the enemy had guns on our right flanks and that the troops on his immediate right were retiring. We had got no orders and didn't want to go, but Dick said that if his right was left in the air he must retire and would let us know. Shortly after, he reported that he was retiring and most reluctantly Toppin gave us the order to go too. We got out in good order, though the men were somewhat overeager to go, and got back about 1,000 yards into the village, which was being shelled.

There we were met by a staff officer who ordered us back again to our trenches, so we went without any hurry or confusion but it was jumpy work walking over the open field. Fortunately we were not expected and were able to reach our trenches without being molested, though a heavy shellfire was opened on us very soon afterwards.

We found some men of the (I think) Worcestershire Regiment, occupying our trenches and it galled me horribly to return under those conditions and I swore terribly at whoever it was who had originated the order to retire.

An hour or so later we got a genuine order to retire through a factory yard and to form up on the road beyond. This order got to us before it got to the Colonel who we found on the road asking what the ***** we were doing. However, we got the official order shortly afterwards with a further order that we were to cover the retirement of the Brigade and the information that the Germans were already in the trenches we had vacated.

There was some confusion on the road and very little field of fire in any direction and it looked very like the end. We built a very hasty barricade across the road and lined up behind it with drawn revolvers expecting every minute to be rushed.

Why the Huns failed to come on I still can't imagine. For about half an hour we hung on there listening to the roar of the battle all round us and getting occasional bullets splattering on our barricade. We, or at any rate I myself, expected every minute to be the last.

The confusion behind us caused by the troops of every unit going back made matters seem more hopeless. Presently however, the confusion cleared away and seeing no sign of the oncoming enemy we went back about 200 yards and took up a position where we had a rather better field of fire. We were not there long, before we got orders to clear right back for about a mile into open country and dig ourselves in. I shall never forget the feeling of relief when we got into open country again and were able to see something of what was happening.

On the way back we passed General Shaw who congratulated me on being the last person to leave the canal at Mons, and said we had all done splendidly. Being very sick at having to retire and being also very hungry, hot and tired, I thought he was being sarcastic and thought it in very bad taste on his part. It was not till some days later that I realised that the dear old boy meant every word he had said. He must have thought me very ungracious.

We dug ourselves hasty entrenchments and lay in them for about an hour and then went back another mile and formed up with the rest of the battalion in a stubble field. We made ourselves some protection in case we were shelled and lay down for a three hour rest.

We could see signs of the enemy and occasionally they threw shells pretty near us but not into us. I got a wash at a farm and some kind person gave me a biscuit and a bit of chocolate (I had given all I had on me to the men) as we were not allowed to light fires to cook ourselves some soup cubes.

At about 4.00pm we fell in again and marched away out of Belgium, crossing the frontier at Rinette. I was sent on ahead on a bicycle to a place called Houdain to take over billets for the battalion and to meet the transport there.

I got to the village and found a gunner there with the transport and with him got a sup of ale from the priest. The inhabitants were full of reports of the muchly feared Uhlans who were it seemed all around us, and sure enough we soon got word from some of our own cavalry and also received orders to leave Houdain and go into a divisional bivouac at a place called Bermeries.

Once again therefore I mounted the old push bike and pedalled slowly to Bavai. From this place to Bermeries bicycling was almost impossible as the road was blocked by regiments, guns, transport and fleeing natives with their lares and pennants packed into every kind of cumbersome vehicle.

On arrival at Bermeries I found some staff officers with lanterns (it was quite dark by now) and went up to one of them to ask where was our bivouac. To my joyful surprise I found I was speaking to an old friend in Col. Roger Boyel, late of the Munster Fusiliers.

He told me whereabouts we were to bivouac and once more I plodded along in the dark. I fell into one ditch and had one or two minor accidents of that sort but eventually found our field. I also picked up the transport again and the quartermaster, and we got a fire going ready for the battalion when it came along – which it did at about midnight – most of it being as tired and cross as I was myself.

I got rid of the soup without persuasion and had a sup of it myself and was quite ready for it too having had only a biscuit since breakfast on Sunday (now Monday pm!) We lay down on and under the corn sheaves where we halted and got some sleep but it was a cold night and our field was a damp one.

25th August

Retreat from Mons sees rearguard action at Landrecies. Austria-Hungary declares war on Japan.

J F Williams

We hear of the fall of Namur. Plenty of people to say, 'I told you so.' A few transports leave most days.

Tudor St John

I woke up at daylight and found that a certain amount of rations had arrived and got some breakfast and also a tin of bully and some biscuits to go on with. We fell in at 5.00am and continued on our march via Le Quesney and Le Cateau to Inchy which we reached at about 6.00pm.

On the way we heard shooting behind us now and then but did not do any ourselves and we saw a very pretty fight in the air. This fight was between a Taube and two of our aeroplanes, and lasted for quite an hour. Time and again the Taube would try and get back to its own line but each time one of our fellows would head him away while the other manoeuvred for position above him.

Eventually our men were successful and forced him to land evidently in a very crippled condition. He came down about a half mile from us and as he came over us we gave him a welcome from our rifles too.

Our mounted people rode up to where he fell but when they got there they found the Taube in flames and no Germans to be seen. When we got to Le Cateau a heavy thunderstorm broke and we all got drenched. Again I was sent on to take over billets and rode from our village to another on beastly greasy roads and a rather flat tyre.

At each village we found other troops and eventually returned to the village of Inchy where we got quite cosy billets in a big barn. We also got into the local schoolmaster's house where we were given hot water to wash in and a bang up supper too with some muchly appreciated wine and beer.

We got to bed at 10.00pm with orders to turn out at 2.00am and to sleep in our equipment, which we did. As soon as we turned out we got the order to turn in again and stand to arms as usual at dawn.

26th August

Battle of Le Chateau. French and British Commanders confer at St Quentin but fail to agree a co-ordinated strategy. Britain obtains code book the Russians captured from a German ship, enabling Britain to break German naval codes.

J F Williams

Four ships leave in the morning, destination unknown. Probably Calais or Ostend. I think they have taken Marines with them but nothing official yet.

Tudor St John

We turned out again at daybreak and had some breakfast and were told that we were to dig ourselves in near by. We fell in at 5.00am and began by flattening a cornfield by marching over it.

We then went to our digging area and took over the site of our trenches. Before we had begun to dig we were told that our company were to be in reserve that day so we retired to a sunken road some 300 yards in the rear where was gathered all the 1st lines' transport.

We lay down under cover of the embankment and I went to sleep again but was woken up again by the explosion of a shell. Apparently a Taube had found the sunken road and the enemy was shelling it.

I clung very close to the ground and got off but we had several causalities in the company including Dorman Smith who got a bullet through his arm. We bound him up and sent him and the other wounded away and buried the dead.

The transport shifted from our neighbourhood to a safer place. When we had done all this Toppin informed me that he was hit too and asked me to bind up his arm. He had quite a nasty wound near his elbow and I bound him up as well as I could. Later on we got an R.A.M.C. man to fix him up better.

We lay there most of the day, nothing much seemed to be happening where we were except occasional bursts of rapid fire from our trenches and a shell or two from the enemy. There was much commotion away on our right and a hot fight seemed to be going on there.

At about 4.30pm we got orders to vacate the position and to fall back. As my company had been in reserve all day we were naturally ordered to cover the retirement of the remainder of the battalion although as luck would have it we were the only company who had suffered any causalities.

However those who were not hit had had a very easy day and those who were hit were either buried or back in the ambulance so far as we knew. As soon as the rest of the Battalion had got away one half of my company went back to another position, I remained to cover their retirement. The Germans advanced to within 1,000 to 1,200 yards of us and we blazed away at them, but didn't seem to do much damage as the enemy was in pretty extended order. When I saw that the other half of the Company were back in position we went quietly back too, stopping in the road to examine and empty some ammunition boxes.

When we had got back a bit Toppin signalled us to halt and came up to us and said that Booth had been left behind in his trenches, no one having told him to retire. I collected some men and went back again to help him out. As we got back however we found him coming away and we all retired together going in open order for about 500–600 yards across fields.

We then joined up with the other half of the company on a road and proceeded through a tiny village (Thourvilles) very knocked about by shellfire to where the Battalion was formed up. As soon as we joined up the whole battalion moved off in close order and we marched along behind a belt of trees till we were about another mile back when we again halted. Here we came upon other troops who told us unpleasant stories of defeat, which seemed to be more or less corroborated by the numbers of small bodies of straggling troops, which kept passing us.

As it seemed we were to wait there for some time, my Company was sent off to take up a protective position, which we did. We had a good view of the country from where we lay and could see the Germans all over and around the position, which we had left while the whole countryside was well besprinkled with burning farms etc.

Now and again shells would burst in our neighbourhood but none very close to us. It was a heavy heart I had in me during the time that we lay there and to me the future looked very gloomy indeed. But still nothing happened and presently we were able to form up as rear guard to the Battalion and to continue our march.

It now became a question of daylight. There was only about an hour to go before it was dark and if the Germans did not catch us by then there was a good chance of our getting away under cover of night. It was an exciting hour. Progress was slow owing to the blocked roads and checks were frequent. We closed up our rear guard but I don't know what protection we had in rear of us except of course the cavalry who were apparently in close touch with the enemy.

Occasionally we saw little groups of mounted men on our flanks but could never make out whether they were friend or foe. As dusk began to fall a wet mist came down which served the double purpose of wetting us and hiding us from view. When the darkness became complete we halted in a tiny village. At first we thought it was an ordinary halt due to a minor block on the road. As we stood there in the dark not a sound was to be heard baring an occasional shuffle as some man shifted his equipment or the unique splash of the inevitable and inexhaustible expectoration for which soldiers must be world famous.

As time went on and no advance was made we sat or lay down in the road and most of the men slept and snored uneasily. They were too tired and scared to talk though this didn't prevent one or two thoughtless, selfish idiots from striking a match to light his fag with. This was invariably followed by the low murmur of the stream of suitable invective uttered by the offender platoon or Company Commander.

It is an extraordinary thing that in spite of explanations of the cause of the order forbidding it, one would constantly find some men who would risk the safety and lives of the entire army corps by lighting a match. In doing so, they would disclose our very precarious position to the enemy rather than curb their craving for the pernicious woodbine. I could not sleep myself. I was tired enough but it was cold and a steady drizzling rain made slumber in the open impossible, and I did not like to go away from the column to a cottage in case a move was made while I slept.

27th August

British fall back from St. Quentin. Ostend occupied by British force of Marines.

J F Williams

It is known almost for certain that the four ships had almost 200 Marines in them. War news doesn't look very bright. Papers seems emphatic about our good position and that the best strategy is being used and almost that a withdrawal was expected. Russian news looks good.

General painting and repairs to the ship. I wonder if the High Fleet will move if the Germans get to Calais. They may try getting troops across from here but it sounds very risky but there is no knowing what they will try.

People are getting quite into this sort of routine though some are annoyed with the painting and scraping as it does not seem like war work. It can be especially irritating when we all down tools to give a transport a good send off. Japan has joined the war now but I can't decide whether this will be a good thing in the end. Italy looks like she will make some sort of move.

Tudor St John

Sometime past midnight we again marched and made a slow though steady progress till an hour before daybreak when we were given an hours halt. This time I made no bones about it, but lay down on the wet grass by the roadside and rain or no rain went straight off to sleep.

I had nearly been asleep all the time we were marching and had imagined all sorts of weird sights. All the time I thought there was a bright light about a mile in front of us and another a mile behind us. I was also quite certain that on each side of us was a broad sheet of water which followed the road all the way along. Beyond those waterways were troops both mounted and dismounted.

At daybreak we fell in again. I felt very stiff and tired and was surprised to see no water and no other troops, while so far as could be seen there was nowhere that could have furnished the bright light referred to.

We marched slowly at first and then halted for about half an hour and joined the rest of the division with whom we continued to march. All along the road we saw signs of a hurried retreat. Overturned motor and other wagons and dead horses were strewn by the roadside while numbers of fed-up and exhausted men sat looking disconsolate.

The sight of these men had the effect on our men of making them wonder why they were foot slogging along instead of sitting down on a nice bank. They all of them seemed to become suddenly exhausted and unable to keep up, and for now on for a couple of days my life became a burden for me as I was all the time urging, persuading and even kicking men on. It was no good to explain to them that there was no choice but going on or falling into the hands of the Germans, they simply did not believe me.

Another evil with which we had to contend was the kindness of the inhabitants of the villages through which we passed. They all did what they could for the men in the way of offering them fruit and drink, the trouble being that there was not enough to go round and the men used to have a regular sort of free fights for it.

This all tended to check the pace of a column, which was stretching along the road for 10 or 12 miles. Here again mere issuing and reiterating orders was of no avail and I was continually using physical force as well to get the men back to ranks. The sight of the Regiment in front filling every village and wolfing everything to be got, while ours had to march along in proper formation must have been highly galling to our wild north country pitmen reservists, who really, on the whole, behaved very well indeed.

We plodded on through a hot morning always within earshot of gunfire behind us and at midday were halted for two hours in a farmyard. This was with the idea of letting us cool and eat a meal, but as we had nothing to eat the reason became rather an anomaly. However we were glad of the rest and as there was a fine well we got a good drink and were able to wash a bit. We fell in at the appointed hour but were told that we were to let the rest of the army through and to again act as rear guard, so we fell out again.

Before the column had passed through, shells began to burst round and about us so we cleared out and made a demonstration away from the road. This, in conjunction with the manoeuvres of our divisional cavalry had the desired effect and the shelling ceased.

When the column had gone through us we fell back and took up a commanding position about a mile behind and on the other side of the road. While lying here we saw some German artillery trot leisurely onto a plain at the foot of our hill, and as leisurely, proceed to unlimber.

They were too far away for any fire from us to touch them and we could not get close enough to them without exposing ourselves in the open. How we longed for a gun for they didn't take any trouble to get their horses undercover, but most of our very meagre artillery had been knocked out at Frameris and Le Cateau and we were not risking any of the precious remainder in a rearguard action.

The German gunners lolled around for a time and as no enemy soldiers presented themselves as a target they fired incendiary shells into all the farms within range. Very fine farmsteads they were too, one of them being in fact quite a small chateau and it made one furious to see them so wantonly burned.

We hung on in this place for about an hour and a half and then carried on the retirement in open order. At one place I had to take up a position behind a wall which formed one of the boundaries of a large paddock in which were two old horses and an ancient cow. There was a similar wall at the other end of the field and along the top too.

In order to facilitate a retreat if necessary I opened the gate at the far corner. Shortly afterwards I noticed that this gate was shut and found on examining it that it was padlocked. I looked about and saw the farmer walking away and called to him to come and open it. He came but refused to open it on account of the horses.

However the sight of my revolver, which I drew with the intention of blowing in the lock, made him change his mind in a hurry and he unlocked it. To make it quite safe I got some men and we removed the gate altogether.

We were not long in this position and when we had gone back another half mile or so, we came upon the rest of the Battalion that were halted by the roadside. We waited here to let the cavalry get out to a ridge some distance away on our right. While waiting the Colonel who was on his horse behind the Battalion suddenly called out, 'retire double.'

The ensuing panic showed just how jumpy everyone was. I myself thought for the moment that the enemy was on top of us. However we rushed to our men and got them into order again. I found out that the Colonel's horse whilst grazing by the roadside had shoved its nose or foot into a nest of hornets and the Colonel was afraid that the brutes would attack the men who were rather close to them. We saw lots of these hornets but I did not hear of any casualties resulting from them.

As soon as the mounted troops had secured the ridge we went on again and after a few miles march we passed through a line of out posts. The sight of the Scotsmen furnishing the outpost and troops digging themselves in gladdened our hearts for it looked like a night in bed. This, however, was not to be; though we were allowed to rest till midnight.

Our commissariat department had commandeered 4 or 5 sheep by the wayside and these we now killed and made a meal of them for the men with a very small ration of bread and biscuit too. Having seen the men supplied, we officers departed on a foraging expedition of our own.

Several hundred officers seemed to be on the same tack but dear wily old Toppin had as usual got the weather side of them and had found a very nice little cottage. Here we were provided with an excellent meal of roast duck and omelette and some bottles of wine. Neither had he forgotten our past scarcity of provisions and when he rode away there was a bottle of cherry brandy in each holster, while the weight of a couple of ducks slung on one side of his saddle was balanced on the other side by a goose. After our meal, we went back and lay down in the street for an hour or two and got some sleep.

28th August

Kaiser orders advance on Paris. Battle of Heligoland – German cruisers Mainz, Koln, and Ariadne sunk. HMS Arethusa suffered significant damage during battle.

Tudor St John

At midnight we again fell in as ordered, but it was an hour and a half before we got away from the town so slow was the rate of march at starting. During one of those weary halts when one didn't know if one would go on the next minute or not, there was nearly a panic owing to a gun or wagon team behind us stampeding in a narrow street. At once the report flew up the column that the enemy cavalry were charging us and it was significant of the state of our nerves that no one doubted the report for a moment.

Certainly everyone I am sure was greatly relieved when we got out of the streets into open country where one had some chance if attacked. We marched till daybreak when we had an hours halt and I got a little more sleep. I had already several times gone to sleep while marching and had found myself in the ditch.

I gave up trying to drive men back to the ranks when they fell out; they knew what was in store for them by now as well as I did and I knew the agony they must be suffering from their feet. Many of them had raw heals and toes from the hard marching we had done. Not many gave in absolutely. Some would fall out but at the next halt they would come limping in again.

We felt a bit better after our halt. The pace to begin with had been killing. I don't know who was to blame for this but Gott Strafe him whoever he was.

Soon after restarting we came to a paved roadway along which we painfully hobbled. I can't call it anything else. I don't suppose we were doing 2 miles an hour. I myself was suffering from an abscess on my toe, which felt like hot knives at every step. Toppin lent me his horse every now and again, which relieved things a bit, but at last I could stand it no longer. As our doctor had been killed at Frameries I took over my own case and removed the offending abscess with my pocket knife and felt much more relieved after doing so.

We were told that our destination was Ham and this place we reached at about 10 or 11 o'clock. While waiting outside Ham, what I call the 'Incident of the Horse' occurred. At Le Cateau or Frameries, I forget which, the company cob became a casualty, but the company groom with memories of S. Africa MI service still fresh in his mind had annexed the mount of a gunner trumpeter which he stated was without an owner and running loose.

As we passed along a column of transport and artillery halted by the roadside, Toppin had observed some sleepy gunners become suddenly wide awake and very interested in his mount. He had at once crossed to the near side of the column and dismounting had covered the harness and as much as possible of the horse with rugs and coats but it was no good.

A short time after we halted a Major of the R.F.A. strolled up and identified the animal and we had to hand it over. However the said Major was very good about it, and produced a much more comfortable cob which his trumpeter had annexed from a farm house, and handed this animal with a plain saddle and bridle over to Toppin.

There was a big block on the road crossing the narrow bridge over the Somme, and as we were likely to be held up for some time we were told off to prepare defence works. The lot of the Battalion fell to a cemetery, which we put into a state of defence.

My Company on this occasion being in reserve we decided to cook our goose. We also brought a ration of chickens for the men and some rabbits. Before we had got the grub properly cooked however we were off again and our goose was wasted, though luckily the men got their meal finished in time. I got a little food as we swapped half our goose with the sergeants for a tin of bully and half a tin of jam, and we got an issue of half a biscuit each.

As soon as we were over the bridge it was blown up, much to our relief, as we had heard gun fire in the distance behind us which sounded to be coming much closer as time went on. We crawled along all that afternoon till about 6.00pm we reached Crisolles where we went into billets which I had ridden on to take over on the Colonel's horse which saved me couple of miles of the weariest march I had ever done. We covered 62 miles in 48 hours and I never want to do half of it again.

At Crisolles I was able to buy two pairs of socks and when after a sumptuous repast Toppin and I turned into real and comfortable beds I threw the old ones out which were ******, but never mind what they were. Suffice it to say that I threw them hastily out of the window and they fell on to a soldier sleeping in the garden, who if rumour is truth never recovered consciousness again.

H M Wilson
HMS Euryalus

Dear Mother,

Thanks very much for your letters. I hope you got mine all right. Things aren't very promising are they? The Germans will probably land in England. We go to sea tomorrow Saturday. I expect we shall get blown up, as we are sure to go where there are mines. This is much better than the Cumberland as some of the Dartmouth and Osborne masters are onboard.

Your loving son,

Hubert

29th August

British retire to Compiegne-Soissons. Germans occupy Amiens.

Tudor St John

Next day the Battalion was detailed to furnish outposts and I was sent to guard a certain road at a certain spot. It was rather an important spot so the Colonel came with me to see if the two platoons I was to have were enough. We essayed a short cut to the place and got into a spinney with thick undergrowth. Through the middle of the spinney ran quite a deep though a not very wide stream. We could not see any sign of a bridge and were preparing to wade, a performance I regard with anything but delight, when my eye caught a depression in the undergrowth that looked like and proved to be a track. Moreover the track led us to a small footbridge over which we crossed dry shod.

We reconnoitred the position and decided what to do with it when I saw troops about fi a mile out beyond it. We at once thought they were Germans but on bringing our glasses to bear upon them saw that they wore kilts which reassured us. We found that they were a Company from another Brigade, also sent to furnish outposts at this spot.

We decided magnanimously to allow them to do the work and were just starting off back when another company from another division appeared bent on the same errand. They approached us in battle order under the impression that we were Germans. We left them to make up their own minds what to do and took our departure to join up with the Battalion at another place in a nice wood where I lay for the rest of the day in reserve and peace.

In the course of the afternoon we saw another fight in the air. This time between a Taube and one little French Monoplane. The little fellow flew round and over and under and past the big bird like Taube, firing away at it but the big one sailed on serenely and got clear away to its own lines.

At about 5 o'clock we were attacked by some mounted Huns with a couple of horse artillery guns. I do not think they were anything but a strong patrol for our fire drove them off with very little difficulty.

At dusk we were told that the column had safely crossed the Oise at Noyous and that we were to follow on leaving the Lincolnshire Regiment to block the road after we had gone through. We marched away and at about midnight crossed the Ois – the bridge being blown up as soon as we were over.

Alfred Williams

Log Book entries. I think my grandfather must have copied this from a book or newspaper.

'I rejoice with you in Wilhelm's first victory. How magnificently God supported him' (Telegram from Kaiser to Crown Princess)

The Kaiser and God
By Barry Pain (1867–1928)

Led by Wilhelm as you tell,
God has done extremely well:
You with patronising nod
Show that you approve of God
Kaiser face a question new –
This – does God approve of you?
Broken pledges, treaties torn
Your first page of war adorn;
We on fouler things must look
Who read further in that book
Where you did in the time of war
All that you in peace forswore
Where you, barbarically wise
Bade your soldiers terrorise
Where you made – the deed was fine –
Women screen your firing line
Villages burned down to dust
Torture, murder, bestial lust,
Filth too foul for printers ink
Crime from which the apes would shrink
Strange the offerings that you press,
On the God of Righteousness
Kaiser when you'd decorate
Sons or friends who serve your state

Not that Iron Cross bestow
But a cross of wood and so –
So remind the world that you
Have made Calvary anew
Kaiser when you'd kneel in prayer
Look upon your hands and there
Let that deep and awful strain
From the blood of children slain
Burn your very soul with shame
Till you dare not breathe that name
That now you glibly advertise
God as one of your allies
Impious braggart you forget –
God is not your conscript yet
You shall learn in dumb array
That his ways are not your ways
That the mire through which you trod
Is not the high white road of God
To whom whichever way the combat rolls
We, fighting to the end, commend our souls.

30th August

General Kluck moves German army north of Paris, attempting to surround and kill retreating allies.

Tudor St John

We hoped we would get a rest then, but no, we plodded on all throughout the night except for one long block on the road when the colonel produced some soup squares. We got a small fire going and I got two delicious mouthfuls of hot soup that the keen night air made very acceptable. By an hour after sun up we were on the move again and we marched along by the lanes and byroads till noon when we were given a long halt. To our joy we were provided with some rations while

Toppin rode on and found a little shop where he got some potted meats and delicacies of that sort. While halted we were officially informed that the situation was considerably relieved and that the need for all the strenuous marching which we had experienced was gone and we should be able to take things easier in future. This cheered us up a lot as we had always been led to suppose that the French were to come in on our left but had failed to do so hence our retreat and we now gathered that they had come in and all was gas and glitter once more.

After resting for some hours we again fell in and continued our march expecting every few minutes to reach our billets. Hour succeeded hour however and it was nearly 7.00pm when we reached the Aisne at Vic-sur-Aisne. As we crossed the bridge there I asked a staff officer how far it was to our billets.'Just up the road and round the corner on the left,' was his reply. We plodded on for about another two miles and found our billets was a lovely big chateau with room for the entire battalion in the large outhouses and we had visions of great comfort for the officers, lots of good food and wine too. Alas it was not to be. To our great wrath and indignation we were told that the arrangements for the billets had been changed. The Divisional Staff Officer motoring round had spotted the chateau and had obtained leave to appropriate it for the staff, in place of the hotel in which they were quartered in town.

What was more galling to us was the fact that we could not take the hotel as it was out of our brigade area but had to trudge on over another two miles to the top of a high hill which was the far extremity of the area. The brigadier had purposely put us in the chateau, which was the Brigade Headquarters too, because we had done most of the hard work, and it was the best and also nearest billet. When we got to the top of the hill we had to search for the billets in the dark. Luckily we found a small chateau which could take nearly all the Battalion and which could provide a bed for each officer which was a joy. The owners were there arranging it as a hospital, and they gave us an excellent dinner with champagne and cigars galore.

W H Carver

At around 7.30pm the telephone rang in the home of my great-grandfather, Major William Carver. It was the Lord Lieutenant of the East Riding, Lord Nunburnholme, who had been meeting Kitchener in London earlier in the day.

The outbreak war had created a growing need for a new army. It would have to be a civilian army made up of volunteers, and Lord Nunburnholme had been handed the job of raising the first service battalion in Hull.

Major Carver was the man he called on for assistance. He was a personal friend and also recently re commissioned into the army after serving 17 years in the militia. He was anxious that his service be used to the full and agreed to start work the following day on building what was to be known as the seventh Hull Battalion and then later on the 10th Battalion, East Yorks Regiment.

Notes from The Trench, *page 11.*

31st August

W H Carver

Carver organises for posters to be printed and distributed around Hull inviting men of a commercial background to join up.

Notes from The Trench, *page 12.*

Tudor St John

The next day we made a quiet and uneventful march only doing about 15 miles. The Brigade was finding the rear guard as usual but we were not called upon to do anything but march along. I began to have a weakness of my innards on this day but not very seriously inconvenienced thereby, though I did not feel as fit and well as I had felt so far. We passed through Villier Cotteret where we were able to buy some bread, and were billeted that night in a sugar factory at Vanciennes. Just before we were arriving at our billet we noticed a lot of men were suddenly overcome with heat and fatigue. We also noticed that we had just passed an estaminet, (a small bar or cafe). I went up to one poor man who had fallen out and was lying by the roadside apparently in extremes with his cap over his face. On lifting the cap I was met by a very bright and hopeful eye and a most healthy and hearty countenance, the property of one of the biggest scoundrels in the Battalion. I said nothing to him but passed on knowing that Toppin with the provost party were waiting round the corner behind us with a view to raiding the estaminet when the Battalion had passed along to its billet. The raid was a most successful one yielding some twenty or thirty exhausted ones including my bright-eyed corpse.

1st September

Kitchener meets Sir John French in Paris, orders him to co-operate with the French and give up plans to withdraw BEF from France. French is shocked by losses incurred by BEF, as it is the only army available to defend Britain's shores. He fears BEF will be wiped out defending France.

W H Carver

W H Carver leaves home for Wenlock Barracks in Hull to find the first civilians waiting outside to join up. My Great Aunt, Patricia, his 14-year-old daughter, went with him and remembers seeing around twenty or thirty men, waiting for his arrival. She recalls he was so pleased there were at least some. As it turned out 700 enlisted that day and more forms had to be printed to accommodate the numbers.

Notes from The Trench, *page 14.*

Tudor St John

I spent that night in an empty garage on a heap of straw and early the next morning we had to take up a position to cover the retirement of the division which went right through us. We stuck on there for eight or ten hours and heard heavy fighting going on to the west of us all the time but did not see much ourselves.

We had to get back through a big wood which was slow work and very alarming work too and it was not until about 9.00pm that night that we reached our billets. I slept that night in a very dirty cottage and was feeling very seedy as I had so felt all day. The inhabitants had almost entirely deserted the village and we could get no food other than the rations we had with us.

H M Wilson
Spurrier's Sun & York Hotel
Chatham

Dear Mother,

Thanks very much for all the papers, chocolates and collars. We came in here to coal and do engine room repairs. This is the swell part of the establishment. This is more or less what we have been doing. We went to the North Sea about Aug 5th and patrolled with the fleet marines and destroyers.

We came into coal about the 10th and then went out to the Isle of Wight. We joined up with the second Battle Fleet and patrolled between Dover and Calais. The battle ships went further down. This was to let the Expeditionary Force get across. When we came in again we coaled and fitted up as the flagship of Admiral Christian. He came aboard about the 18th and we went to sea patrolling off Holland.

One night about 2am while I was on watch we got a wireless sending us to Ostend. We got there in the morning but the authorities asked us to move off. So we went back again to our old job.

We went into coal last Sunday week. I decoded a wireless on Tuesday evening ordering us to embark Marines, destination unknown. They came aboard on Wednesday morning and we took them over to Ostend that day at 4am. That evening we left and on Thursday heard there was going to be a 'drive'.

We knew our destroyers were in action at about 8am on Friday off Heligoland. We met four of them in the afternoon. The Laurel, Lurcher, Liberty and Laertes. The Liberty was taken in tow straight away. We lowered a couple of boats. I was in one taking the wounded across to the Bacchante. They say they had torpedoed the York.

They had eleven killed and a good many wounded. They were under fire from the forts and ought to have been exterminated. The German shooting must have been bad. A very smart move landing these Marines. They will probably go to Ostend.

As midshipmen we keep night watches, 12 to 2 or 2 to 4 is the worst. If we are attacked we control the searchlights. We do general quarters, i.e. stations in action everyday. We did some practise firing the other day off the German coast. The same as in action but with solid shell fire at a target. Our shooting is quite fair and things are much better. We live in a bit of a pigsty and we get 2/9 a day. Princely pay? It covers my mess bill as I only drink beer. There are about 30 officers and about 100 more men than necessary. So there will probably be lots of laughter. I don't think it is any good sending anything.

I notice people walk about with flags in their buttonholes but don't dream of volunteering. The Arethusa had only been in commission three days and was hit in four places so she had very bad luck. I got a photo of her being towed in by the Hogue. I don't want this letter to be read by anyone but you and Father or Leslie. It hasn't been censored. I hope everything is all right at Barmere.

Your loving son,

Hubert

2nd September

Germans reach the River Marne.

W H Carver

With enough recruits to form a Battalion, recruitment stops and the training starts. Several retired army officers had been among those that joined up and were roped in to help Major Carver as well as other experienced members of his own family. These were just the first few of the 20,000 men from Hull who would come forward to join up in the next six months. Now began a long period of training and instruction that would last around a year. There was a chance this might be cut if there was a need for troops in France.

Notes from The Trench, *page 15.*

Tudor St John

Next morning we made our usual early start and got off, for a wonder, very nearly at the hour named. As a rule we would be ready to march at 4.00am and not move till 6.00am but this morning we got away quite soon as we were leading the column. The result was that many of the men had not been able to fill their water bottles, the only supply being one pump.

I felt rotten all that day and could hardly get along at all. The heat was intense and my complaint very troublesome. We did not march very far, about 12 miles, I think, and halted in a village Penchard about a mile north of Meaux, which we reached early in the afternoon.

During this march we came upon a company of what looked like, I think, Gordon Highlanders, strung out as an advanced guard. We asked them where the rest of their battalion was and were told that they were all that was left of an entire Battalion.

I at once secured a bed and turned in but as we had so much time the colonel took the opportunity to tell off malefactors and as I was evidence against several culprits, I had to turn out again and attend. We got a good dinner that night, a real five course one, but I was not feeling inclined for food at all.

3rd September

Germans begin to cross the Marne.

Tudor St John

Next day we crossed the Marne at Meaux, all the bridges being destroyed after we had crossed. We went some seven or eight miles south and east of Meaux and halted our Battalion, being told off to furnish day and night outposts. Putting these out took up most of the rest of the day and I must have covered a good many miles visiting various sentry groups.

Our cavalry patrols came through us with information to the effect that the enemy had crossed the Marne and that we might expect to be exterminated at any moment. They could not get in to touch with the column on our right and also intimated that they had no intention of doing anything else except get behind us as soon as they could. The prospect was not alluring but I did not think it as bad as the horsemen made it out to be.

I sent a man or two on bicycles to find our right which they soon did and my own patrols saw nothing of the Germans. My wretched disease kept me awake nearly all night otherwise the night passed without incident.

4th September

Belgians open the dykes and prevent German advance on Antwerp. Battle of the Marne begins.

Tudor St John

Next day we remained on out post duty till about 5.00pm when we returned to the Brigade bivouac being relieved by the Scots Fusiliers. I got a dish of hot bacon and potatoes cooked in a field and lay down in a corn stack as soon as I could. At 10.00pm we were aroused, and, leaving our campfires burning we started on our last trek south. All that night we marched steadily through sleeping towns, over rivers through forests and vineyards all looking very ghostly in the moonlight. We covered about 28 miles and then halted at a village called Chartres about 15 miles south east of Paris. We were very crowded here for billeting space but Toppin found room for us in the priest's house where I got the priest's bed and turned in.

5th September

The British and French had been retreating since arriving at Mons but now all retreats are ceased. HMS Pathfinder torpedoed by Germans. First battle of the Marne halts German advance.

W H Carver

With nearly 1000 men signed up, they now undergo the army medical exam.

Notes from The Trench, *page 18.*

Tudor St John

I got a few hours fevered sleep filled with fearsome dreams of defeat and catastrophe and when I awoke I felt so bad that I went and found our doctor, who told me my temperature was nearly 104, and took me away to a field ambulance. Here I was doped and put to bed on a stretcher under a hayrick.

6th September

General offensive by French and British. Germans checked at Verdun – the most southerly point of their advance.

Tudor St John

Next morning I was put into a wagon with a bundle of straw to lie upon and told I should stop there till there was a chance of sending me to a railhead and from there to a base hospital. I lay in the transport park, all day. Fortunately we were packed near to our wagons and I got my own kit out and had a wash and a shave (first for a fortnight). While lying in the park a Taube flew over us and dropped three bombs but its aim was bad and no harm was done.

That night we shifted north again and after being jolted about all night I found I was back with the battalion again. I asked if I could not rejoin them as I felt better but was told not. I walked over to see them in the morning but felt so weak that I quite realised that the doctor was right.

At about midday I was told that a motor convoy was just going to a railhead and so I said goodbye and departed. I did not think then that I should never again see so many good pals. Toppin, Matthews, Beauchamp, Selby, Dick Gatehouse and Boyd were all dead before that week was out.

My feelings at that moment were very mixed indeed. For one thing I hated to leave the regiment; I felt that we had had our worst time and that things were looking up a bit; I also felt rather renegade to be going to the base. On the other hand, I had undoubtedly had enough for the time being and I was moreover very seedy.

On the whole I must own that the feeling of relief at the prospect of a spell of rest and comfort in safety outweighed the regrets I felt departing and it was by no means a heavy heart which I carried to the motor transport convoy. I collected my belongings from the horsed wagon and found a place on a motor lorry.

We soon were started off on our journey to railhead. I have never experienced a dustier motor ride in my life. I sat in the front seat and there was no wind screen and we were about the 12th lorry in a convoy of 14 going at about 15 to 20 miles an hour on dusty roads. I was like a snowman when I finally reached the station. Here we learnt that a hospital train had departed about a quarter of an hour before and there would not likely be another till next afternoon.

Other convoys came, each bringing its offering of sick and slightly wounded, and we soon collected quite a party. They were a heterogeneous crowd and at first I seemed to be the only officer.

I went up the station platform to try and find somewhere to lay out my bed for the night so as to get cover from the weather, which looked like rain. It was thus that I discovered several other officers. At least an officer or his valise occupied every available place so I wandered out again and as luck would have it I came across an ordnance officer whom I knew. From him I learnt there was an empty ordnance train running sometime that night from Le Mans, which was where the R.T.O. had told me I was to be sent. I went and found the train and made friends with the officer commanding it and ensconced myself and my valise in a 1st class carriage. As I had been told that the train was not going to start for 3 or 4 hours I got out and went in search of food.

I was met by a deputation of men of all sorts of corps who seemed to like my face and who begged me to get them some food. I agreed to do what I could for them and ordered all but four to stay where they were I set out with these and again found my friend of the ordnance corps. He was no use in the way of providing me with food but showed me where food was, in another siding, and pointed out the Supply Officer to me. His refusal to supply us was curt but then he was somewhat young in years and full of importance, his rank being 2nd Lieutenant. I was about to argue the point with him but spotted the arrival of a Supply Staff Colonel to whom I hastened. He was most genial and said that the Supply Officer should give me anything I wanted which was there to be given. I explained that my personal application to the Supply Officer had not met with success and suggested that perhaps his written order would be necessary. 'Not at all,' he replied, 'he is there to supply the fighting units with food when and where it is required and its issue is feasible.' I again approached the young gentleman and proffered my request to be supplied with food for self and men and was again refused curtly so I commanded the lad to accompany me to the Staff Officer. This he objected to doing but fortunately the appearance on the scene of the Staff Officer saved me the trouble of placing him under arrest.

His demeanour soon changed and after the winged words of the Colonel he came with me to the supply train and produced all the grub I wanted. I selected a side of bacon (best cut) and enough bully to last two days with bread, biscuits, jam, tea, sugar and a jar of rum and we returned to our comrades who honoured me with a cheer. I got them to procure me water to wash in and see to the bacon and tea, which they did and when I was abluted and fed I went to sleep. We started on our journey at about 8.00pm. The soft cushions and gentle movement of the train was most soothing and I slept like a cartload of bricks.

H M Wilson
HMS Euryalus

Dear Mother,

Thanks very much for your letter and papers. Yes Admiral Christian was captain at Osborne. We have just arranged our guns for high angle firing. Things seem to be better in France but I don't think we will get them out of there for about six months. When will the Yeomanry go abroad? Have you heard anything about Charlie? Have you told our gardeners to volunteer? I suppose you saw Lord Derby going to sack all his stable men unless they volunteered. Bad luck about the Pathfinder. I remember seeing her off Filey when we were there one summer. I am afraid we will lose a good many more. When does Peggy go back? I hope you got my trunk last night. I hope I shall hear from you soon.

Your loving son,

Hubert

7th September

Germans advance. Battle of Marne continues.

Tudor St John

When I woke up at 7.00am I found that we were still in the environs of Paris. Some Red Cross ladies invaded my carriage and were anxious to dress my wound. I explained that I was not 'blesse', but sick and did not need assistance. So they procured me some hot coffee and a tin containing 5 acid drops and a packet of chocolate.

At the next stop I got out and found several of the other officers I had left at railhead. They had joined my train at the last minute and had spent the night most uncomfortably in a closed truck without straw. I brought them along to the first class carriages and we proceeded on our journey once more.

All day we bumped and shunted and stopped and bumped along again until at about 6.00pm we stopped just outside Le Mans. We thought our journey was just about over but we sat there for over two hours before we again moved and were finally brought to a standstill with a great bump in Le Mans station itself. I got hold of the R.A.M.C. people and after some delay and doubtful consultation was sent in an ambulance up to the hospital in the Bishop's Palace. At first they wanted to send me to a rest camp, but to this I strongly objected. It was raining and dark and I was tired and cross and did not fancy finding my way to a wet camp alone.

The hospital was by no means the home from home that my imagination had pictured it. This was no fault of the R.A.M.C. officials or of anyone to do with it at all. The poor things, owing to the rapidity of the German advance and the Allied retreat, had been obliged to leave their original hospital at Rouen and shift hurriedly south to Le Mans.

I had pictured to myself a bed with soft sheets and, joy of joys, a bath – hot and if possible deep – but at any rate hot and of sufficient size to be taken in a sitting posture. What I found was a good enough bed with hard new canvas sheets and not only was there no big bath but there was no bath at all and no hot water either. True they were putting in a bathroom as quickly as possible but so far as I was concerned I had to content myself with a bucket of cold water. I got over the sheet trouble by sleeping in my fleabag on top of the bed.

8th September

Battle of the Marne continues, forcing Germans back over the river.

Tudor St John

Next morning I was examined by the medical officer who said there was not very much the matter with me so far as he could see and that it was not worth my going down to the base at St Nazaire. I stayed in the hospital at Le Mans for three days and then went out to the Chateau of Le Prince de Lucinge with whom I stayed for ten days.

9th September – 14th September

Pullback ordered to a defensive line along the River Aisne. Battle of the Marne continues with British crossing river in pursuit of Germans.

10th September

Battle of the Marne ends as Germans retreat.

Tudor St John

I shall never forget the kindness of the Prince (Rainier) and his charming American princess. We drove out one rather wet and miserable afternoon, and I had a most glorious hot bath, with all the best imaginable etceteras in the way of bath salts and delicious soaps that go to the making of the modern luxurious bath. Then bed with my dinner brought up to me.

I was still very short of sleep as the noise at the hospital made sleep very difficult, and every night one was awakened by the arrival of convoys, while the hour of being called was never later than 5.00am However that night I made up for a good deal of overdue shuteye and awoke next morning feeling much better.

11th September

Pursuit of Germans from the Marne.

Tudor St John

I must have looked very blooming for the Princesses maid who came in to see me asked if I was wounded and when I told her no, only a sick officer, she remarked 'well you don't look so very sick anyway!!' I stayed at Le Chateau Chardonnieux for 10 days. I felt much better but I was pretty weak and I found that if I walked for more than 3 or 4 miles I got knocked up and the old complaint returned. I used to go to Le Mans every third day to see the doctor who said it was no good sending me back to the battalion until I could do a bit more without breaking down. In spite of the comfort and kindness shown me by all I did not feel happy. I could not feel but that I should be with the regiment again and yet I felt unfit to undergo the half of the fatigues I had been through. I had had my fill of fighting for the time being. I was also filled with longing to see my family again and altogether I became a depressed being. I used to go out with the Prince shooting for the 'pot' partridges, wild duck and even pheasants in September! And in the middle of the walk, (I would not take a gun myself), I would think of my brother officers in the trenches on the Aisne and wonder what they would think of me could they see me.

12th September – 24th October

First Battle of the Aisne. Failing to break German line on the Aisne, Allies try to bypass it to the west. Series of outflanking movements by both sides.

W H Carver

Lieutenant-Colonel Richardson arrives to take over command of the Battalion and Carver steps down to second in command. The borrowed horse is handed over and the Lieutenant addresses the men. The Battalion continues to train locally, practising outpost duty as well as the usual drill and physical training.

Notes taken from The Trench, *page 29.*

13th September

H M Wilson

Dear Mother,

Thanks very much for the waistcoat. We have missed our mail, which is very sickening. They were sent out to us but it was too rough to get them across. We have had it rather wet. I haven't been sick yet but some of us have. The Euryalus is a very good sea boat – much better than the Cumberland. We have had rather a disappointing week. We expected to go into action on Thursday the tenth but the Germans didn't appear as I expect you saw in the papers. I hear the Pathfinder was supposed to have been sunk by a submarine. It has got much colder. I don't know what it will be like in winter. I expect the Kaiser must feel very sick having to retreat after having arrived in France with chargers and champagne already for a triumphal entry into Paris. I don't think we shall stay out here all winter. We shall probably go somewhere else or re commission another ship. Would you send me my 'Germany in the Next War' by Bernhardi. I think Father has got it. It was written in 1911 and describes what Germany would do in the next war. It is practically what she has done.

Your loving son,

Hubert

14th September

Battle of the Aisne begins and continues until Sept 28th.

H M Wilson
H.M.S. Euryalus

Dear Mother,

Thanks very much for your letter. About clothes. Please give everything away except my round jacket and waistcoat. Don't bother about getting my chest home as it is at Chatham and I think it would be better for me to have it there. I am going to go right through it when I have the chance. This job will probably go on for two years or so and it seems to me that by then none of the clothes, which I now possess, will be any good. This also includes sheets and pillow-cases etc. When the war is over I shall have to get a lot of new uniforms because there is nowhere to hang them properly and the way our clothes get washed does not tend to improve them. I got a good many collars, about 1 doz. and some shirts and things like that. They are necessary because this is a flagship. Your last letters about money are probably in the Cressy with our 28 bags of mails. We have just finished coaling and going out this evening. There isn't much new except what I told you yesterday. The Russians certainly came through. They landed at Ostend. The Italian papers got it. That is why the Marines were at Ostend. They were written as soon as the Russians landed.

Your loving son,

Hubert

20th September

H M Wilson

Dear Mother,

We have just come in to coal after a most unpleasant week off the Broad Fourteens and Dogger Bank. We had some hopes of going into action last Wednesday as we heard some German cruisers and destroyers had got out of Emden but as usual it didn't come off. We have had it fairly rough, seas coming over and the whole place flooded which is very unpleasant. Eating is rather an art, as one has to hang onto one's plate's etc., all the time. Of course pouring, howling gales and quite cold.

Most of the officer's cabins got flooded out. They let one send uncensored letters nowadays but they are always delayed so as to make the information valueless. They will only censor very urgent letters, as it was such a long job censoring the whole of the ship's company's. Do you know any patriotic sort of person who would like to send his gramophone along to me? It would be a great asset and I should get my own records down here. One doesn't want a very good one. The Admiralty is going to supply them for the hands. Most people seem to want to know how they can do something. This is one thing they can do. We haven't got any luxuries here I can tell you. We shall probably come in for a refit for a week or so about the first week in October, and I may be able to get two or three days leave. I propose coming back to Barmere if possible. By doing a good deal of night travelling one might get two days or so at home. I have just got your letters. Thanks very much for the book.

Your loving son,

Hubert

Tudor St John

After ten days of this luxurious life of eating and drinking, shooting and motoring (we used to motor to another Chateaux filled with priceless chefs d'oeuvres), I said goodbye to my kindest of hosts and took to what was called 'light duty'! in the base garrison at Le Mans. At first my work consisted of looking after the discipline, pay and interior economy generally of some 1,000 to 1,500 cavalry men of every kind of Corps who were at the base for all sorts of reasons. Some were lost patrols; some were horse casualties (most were there on this count), some stragglers and a few criminals undergoing imprisonment. Some too were sick and slightly wounded.

They were a good lot and gave me no trouble but after I had had them for a day or two they were swept from me to camp some two miles away. I was then given temporary command of the stragglers and casualties belonging to Departmental Corps and the 19th Brigade. The real Commander of this lot was an Officer who had relieved me in 1909 as Camp Staff Officer at Lydd and he had with him my old clerk who had come out with him. He had retired shortly after this and had been put out on this work on the outbreak of war. It was a curious coincidence, which brought us all three together.

While at Le Mans I came into contact with a very good example of the thoroughness with which the Germans laid their plans which was pointed out to me by a member of the French Intelligence Department. Evidently it was part of the German plans to come round the west of Paris and to exploit the valley of the Loire as they did in 1870. About 6 or 8 months before war broke out a commercial traveller came to Le Mans and proceeded to flood every sort of little shop with a patent boot polish called the 'Lion Noir'. This was planted on very advantageous terms to the middleman or retailer on condition that a sign, showing a black roaring lion on a yellow background with a tin of boot polish between its pads, was exhibited outside the shop. In addition to these signs there were posters and larger signs on all the places where posters and advertisements were allowed.

To the casual observer these signs appeared to be exactly alike only of different sizes but if you looked at them a little carefully you would notice that they were by no means so exactly similar. In some the head would be looking one way. Some had tails going straight, some had a twist to them, the legs of the beast were different in some to those in others and so on. The object of all this was a code for directing a rapid raiding party to every sort of place such as the bank, the cathedral and barracks etc. I used to amuse myself following up the various clues to see where I got to. I carried on with light duty for about a fortnight. It was tedious work and the hours 8.00am to 6.00pm were long. Sometimes I would get a break in the monotony by being president of a court martial and I once got myself sent to St. Nazaire with 200 scallywags who were not well enough to go back to the Front within a fortnight's time. I enjoyed my trip to St Nazaire. It took me two days and two nights to get there and back but it was a change in the dreary routine.

22nd September

H.M.S. Aboukir, Hogue and Cressy sunk by German submarine.

23rd September

Battle extends northward along the River Oise.

H M Wilson
HMS Euryalus
Sheerness

Dear Mother,

Thank you so much for the gramophone records. It was very thoughtful of you. We are hiring a gramophone. Isn't it awful about the Aboukir and Co. though of course we expected it. If we had been there they would have got us too. You see they were our squadron. Our patrol had been going on for a month at the same course and speed. We were practically in sight of the Dutch coast. Not far from Emden.

The Germans must have known all about us and could easily have got our speed – that is the great thing in submarine warfare. It may wake the Admiralty up. I don't know what our job will be now. It will alter everything. We got an Admiralty order last night, which says if a ship is torpedoed or strikes a mine the others are to leave her to her fate.

If that had been done yesterday the Cressy and Hogue would be here now. I think most of the cadets doing midshipman are drowned. They probably couldn't stand the exposure. The Aboukir went down in 4 minutes. So only those on deck could jump off it in time.

Most of the snotties were first term at Dartmouth. It is very sickening. Also they had reserve crews so most of them were probably married, and also they were quite useful ships. I should think Christian will get the blame even though he wasn't to blame. The Admiralty will have to put it on someone to appease the general public. Christian is the Admiral of the North Sea patrols.

It is extraordinary that we did not get hit when we were there before. We quite expected it. We were to have gone out on Monday evening but luckily they had to repair our wireless which got damaged by the high winds last time we were out or we should have been with the others, and got hit as well and got sunk probably.

We got a signal at 7 o'clock on Tuesday morning, 'Hogue & Aboukir sinking,' this was from the Cressy. She went down afterwards. I should imagine the Aboukir magazine exploded as her bow was practically blown clean away. They sent out the Lowestoft and a couple of seaplanes. What is so annoying is that the Germans will be so pleased and they have a right to be. Wiping out a whole squadron isn't a bad effort. I don't know what we shall do. We may go abroad or stay here for a bit and do the same job again but they can't be such utter fools as to send us to the same place.

The Germans probably knew far more about our movements than the Admiralty did. I'm afraid there won't be much chance of any leave. This may alter everything. Thanks very much again for the records. I hope it won't be much trouble sending the others. These arrived quite all right. I wouldn't send anything in the food line until we discover what our job will be.

I hope you have got my letters all right by now. I shan't send them that way again. I rather hope we go to a foreign station – it will be warmer anyway. Nothing could be more unpleasant than the North Sea. We had a lot of lightning last week when were in the Broad Fourteens where the other three went down. I shall take great care of the records.

Your loving son,

Hubert

Alfred Williams

At that time the Euryalus (with Admiral Christian on board) was the flagship and the Aboukir, Cressy and Hogue were the rest of the ships in the patrol. One day there was a severe gale and our wireless aerials were damaged. We were flagship and had two tall masts, which gave our wireless extra range. We returned to port because the repairs could only be done while the ship was still. The next morning I had the morning watch in the harbour and a signal came through saying that the Aboukir, Cressy and Hogue had been sunk. I came off watch and announced this, and had to run for my life because they thought I was joking. However it was all too true and it was very lucky for us because we should have been in the Aboukir's place. The squadron had been patrolling up and down the Broad Fourteens, which is an area in the North Sea with a depth of fourteen fathoms. At dawn every day we were in the same place on the same course at the same speed. I believe we were there as a temptation to bring the Grand Fleet out. Instead the Germans sent a submarine and got three cruisers. We were now moved to the Western Approaches near Plymouth and patrolled up and down from Plymouth to Lands End intercepting German merchantmen, (some of these ships did not know the war had started) and we did this for some weeks. Then again a submarine appeared so we scuttled off to the Mediterranean and went to Alexandria where the preparations were being made for the Dardanelles campaign. We then went to Mudros and a thin steel shield was fitted up round the stern sheets of the picket boats and my little steam pinnace, with slots cut for us to see through. I didn't see through mine very well, and had a head on collision with a tug, which was coming round a transport's bow. I thought this was the end of my steam pinnace work. Not so however because on 24th of April 1915 I would help embark the Lancashire Fusiliers.

24th September

Battle ends in stalemate.

26th September – 10th October

Germans take Antwerp.

C Carver

17 year old Christian Carver (nephew of W H Carver) passes fit to enter the Army.

28th September

Trial of Archduke's murderers.

29th September

Turkey enters war on Germany's side.

30th September

Turkey closes the Dardanelles.

1st October

B.E.F. leaves the Aisne to move west and north.

C Carver

Christian Carver leaves Rugby School at the age of 17 and is passed into the R.M.A. in Woolwich.

H M Wilson
Spurriers's Sun and York Hotel
Chatham

Dear Mother,

The Cumberland has been doing quite well in the way of prizes out in Togoland hasn't she? I think we are going down to Sheerness tomorrow but I don't know when we shall go to sea. There is an enquiry going on about the Cressy and Co. so the Admiral has to go to town every day. We shan't go till they finish. Thanks very much for the gloves. Would you please send my blue rug along? I hope we shall go to sea soon and have a show this time.

Your loving son,

Hubert

2nd October

Battles around Arras.

H M Wilson
Sheerness
HMS Euryalus

Dear Mother,

We came down here this morning. The Admiral is in town, as the inquiry hasn't finished yet. I don't know when we shall go to sea. I enclose some photos that have been all taken during wartime. The Silent Navy what! I believe we shall get a bar on our medal for the Heligoland show. Winston has composed some poetry about it, which is only fit to send to Germany.

I think we have got to have Heligoland August 28th 1914 put up in the QD. We weren't there accidentally only we ought to have been. Winston's poem is to be put up on a brass plate in the Arethusa. It will make one the laughing stock of the world. There is lots of work for him to do without writing poetry especially drivel – it is by way of a parody on the Saucy Arethusa.

There is much indignation amongst the powers that be about it. There is also a general vague idea that we are going abroad. I hope it isn't so. I am afraid there isn't much more to say.

Your loving son

Hubert

3rd October

Ypres occupied by Germans.

W H Carver

The four Hull Pals Battalions are marched around the city of Hull for the first time, to everyone's pride and delight.

Notes taken from The Trench, *page 30.*

4th October

H M Wilson

Dear Mother,

I think it is practically certain that we shall be conveying troops from Australia and the Cape. It is very dull here. They sent out four seaplanes and two mother ships today probably to help the minelayers. They come in here to replenish with mines. The inquiry is going on.

There is a lot of conflicting evidence as to whether the Hogue and Cressy were ordered to close by signal. They are getting all the signalmen's evidence. The King and Queen came down to Chatham Hospital yesterday. Just an unofficial visit.

They only give us two hours leave as we are under sailing orders and are supposed to be ready for sea at two hours notice. Thanks very much for writing to Peggy. I will try and let you know what is going to happen.

Your loving son,

Hubert

6th October

H M Wilson

Dear Mother,

The German submarines are on the hop. I think some are in the Channel. The Coquette Destroyer tried to run one down about 2am on Monday off the northern foreland but it dived and they missed it. We moved further up the river yesterday. They are giving our airmen darts about 3" long with very sharp steel points. If they were dropped from any great height they would go straight through your head. The bombs are pretty wicked looking things. I think they are going to drop some on Heligoland.

The minelayers came in again today. One had had a lucky escape as a mine exploded as it was dropped overboard. Luckily no damage was done and no one was hurt. I see the Germans are enrolling an army of boys aged 16. Anything is better than this place but of course it will be deadly dull being at sea for a month or so at a time. We were going to use searchlight yesterday but they cancelled it. I suppose because of the submarines. They could get up the Thames at night if they were lucky. How long was Father home for?

Your loving son,

Hubert

9th October

Tudor St John

By now I was fit enough to go back and got my papers cleared by the P.M.O. But it was not until the 10th of October that I got away as they were about to move the 3rd Division from the Aisne to the north and were not taking drafts just prior to or during the move.

So for a week or more I waited ready to move at an hour's notice or at any rate get away at that notice whether or not I took my kit with me or left it behind at the Hotel Dauphin where I was billeted. The last two nights of my stay I slept in a tent with my draft and one night at midnight got orders to move on the following day at 6.00 am.

13th October

Ypres occupied by Allies.

Tudor St John

We got entrained by 7.00 am. There were several officers of a special reserve battalion going up with a big draft of their regiment and I had a few men of various 3rd Division units. There was also a charming gunner major with his horses and groom.

I soon got my men into the train and took possession of the best of two 1st class compartments allotted to the officers, where I was joined by the major and a young man who informed us that he had been appointed as adjutant of the train. This did not interest me particularly until he invited two of his friends in with him when I pointed out to him that as adjutant it was his job to see that the train was properly filled.

The 5 officers in the carriage in which the Major and I where was one more than the allowance. He was somewhat nonplussed at this but seeing that I meant what I said he went in search of his magic major to support him. This simplified matters as we threw his kit out after him and this saved the arguing that would have ensued to decide who was to go. When his Major appeared, our Major pointed out the facts of the case to him and there the matter ended.

We bumped along all that day and at about 6.00pm we bumped our way into a siding at Rouen. We sat in our carriage there for two hours expecting to be moved or receive some sort of orders. As none were forthcoming some of us went in search of information, climbing over all sorts of obstacles and wondering all the time whether the train would be moved while we were away.

We eventually found the R.S.O. who did not know who we were, where we came from nor to where nor when we were to go. He took steps, however, to telegraph and find out and at about midnight we were informed that we would not move before 5.00am I cadged some hot coffee from the Red Cross sisters at the station ambulance and then bethought me of trying to get hold of my brother Edmund. This I managed to do and he came down and had half an hours chat with me, and at about 2.00am I went back to our train and slept there till 7.00am when I awoke to find we were still at the same old siding.

14th October

Tudor St John

Another expedition to the R.S.O. elicited the news that we would not move till midday so we went off into the town and got shaved and washed and had a dejeuner and then went and had a look at the cathedral. We got back to our train at midday and at 1.00pm we once more banged and clattered off on our way to the Front. We journeyed all that day and also the night.

15th October – 22nd November

First Battle of Ypres. Allied lines extend to coast.

Tudor St John

At 9.00 or 10.00am on the following morning we rolled into Bethune to the accompaniment of artillery fire not so far away. I found Shoubridge on duty at the station and we got a motor to take our valises to the transport park. Shoubridge told me that the Colonel and Herbert were both gone home and that on the previous day General Hamilton had been killed. We were ordered to proceed by route march to join our Brigade who were that day in reserve. We set off feeling very stiff and tired after our long journey and being in reserve we did not hurry. We got to divisional Headquarters at noon and rested there for three hours to cook and eat dinners. We then set off and reached the Brigade Headquarters at about 4.30pm Here, I learned that although the Brigade were in reserve my regiment had been lent to another brigade for a day or two and were else where.

After a cup of tea with Barrett who was acting as ADC to General Shaw, I set off with five other men to find the Battalion. I found the brigade but no one in it that I met could tell me where its Headquarters were nor where my Regiment was. I set off to look and found myself under shellfire so returned and fell in with an intelligent man who was standing outside Brigade Headquarters and didn't know it. However, I thought I would see what was inside the house which looked surrounded with bicycles and orderlies and found the Brigade Major who directed me to my own Battalion Headquarters. I set off to find them in the dark being guided where to branch off by a group of unpleasantly dead horses lying by the roadside.

These I found all right and I also found the quartermaster with the supply convoy and joined onto him. He took me to Headquarters but we found that they had moved on somewhere else. At last at about 9.00pm weary and worn and sad I did roll up and was sent off to my own company, who I found under command of Midford with several utterly strange officers, doing outpost duty. One of the new officers turned out to be my old friend Charles Nunnely who had left the regiment some 8 years previously. I went round the sentries but would not take over command proper till daylight.

16th October

Tudor St John

With the advent of daylight came breakfast and a look round the country. Apparently there had been a good scrap on the previous day and the Germans had left without bothering to collect their lares and penates for there were quite a lot of useful articles in the shape of war material lying about including a number of bicycles which we appropriated.

After breakfast we waited for some time and eventually moved on, the battalion being broken up for various odd jobs as we were in brigade reserve that day. My Company was employed up to 4.00pm in blocking roads on the flank of the advance, which was a dull procedure. Later on in the afternoon our advance troops got into touch with the enemy and for an hour or two there was a lot of noise and much banging of guns but we were not called upon to do anything except sit in a ditch.

At about 5.00pm we went into the little village of Fauguinsart and there we stuck till 7.00pm when I got orders to put out outposts in a certain sector. It took me a considerable time to go over the ground and to choose the positions more particularly as it was all done in the dark and I had only a hazy notion of where the enemy were and no idea of their strength or the probabilities of attack. However, I got them out and also had them fed by midnight and then I got some food myself and dossed down for an hour or two before going round sentries again.

17th October

Tudor St John

At dawn I went round the posts again and found that the most important of all the men were asleep instead of standing to arms, as they should have been doing – the sentries and the N.C.O. I put them back for court-martial knowing of course that it meant certain death for them. It was the most disagreeable duty I had as yet performed. What was the final outcome I don't know for I was knocked out before there was a chance of trying them, though a summary of my evidence and that of my sergeant major who was killed soon afterwards was duly taken.

We got our breakfasts all right that morning but only just in time for at a very early hour we were told to advance to cover the left of the brigade who were advancing on the town of Aubers. I spread the company out into as convenient as possible a formation and we proceeded slowly and cautiously to the foot of the ridge on which Aubers stands. Here I called a halt until I was quite sure that the ridge was clear and could get an idea of the ground on the far side of it. I also collected a few 'bits' of the company, which had gone astray in their endeavour to avoid barbed wire fencing.

We were at the foot of the ridge which was I suppose about 50 feet in height and to the north of Aubers in-between that town and the village of Fromelles. I got the half of the company I was with together and put them under cover and was going on to the top of the ridge where the leading platoon had already arrived where I was unexpectedly fired on from the direction of Fromelles. As I had been told that the French had cleared this village and that there was no one in it excepting perhaps a few wounded Germans I did not think much of this fire to begin with. However it became more intense and as it was very persistent I decided to swing round the rear half company and advance towards Fromelles with the idea of finding out what the bother was about.

As we advanced the fire became heavier and more accurate but I could not see anything to fire at in return. When we were within about 500 yards on the village, I halted and we made ourselves snug while I sent back a signal for supports. We had had eight or nine casualties and I could not yet see a sign of the Germans. The field we were in being ploughed land it was easy to entrench ourselves sufficiently against rifle fire and so far we had not encountered any shellfire. I waited here for an hour or two for the supports I had asked for but none came and eventually I got a message to say I was to stay where I was as the French were going to clear the village.

The next order I got was one to go back myself to interview Yatman. I did not like the idea of this too well but there was nothing for it but to go and so back I went and thanks to bad marksman ship of the Huns who fired at me I got back in safety.

I had expected to be given important orders with regard to the carrying out of a further advance but I found it was only to be asked what steps I had taken to evacuate my wounded!!! It must have been quite obvious that such a thing was impossible until Fremelles was cleared or it became dark. I felt furious at having been called upon to risk my life to answer such an absurd question and showed pretty plainly what I thought about it. I went back to my company and shortly after my return there the French began to clear the village.

If you can imagine the village to be in the middle of a square of which my company formed one side and the French advance an adjacent side, you will see that I was in a position to see a very pretty fight, and I settled down to enjoy myself. In the middle of the village was a church with a spire and on this the French began to range. Two or three rounds were enough to burst shrapnel quite close to the spire and then the real business began. The French Infantry were about 800 yards away from the village and between them and the village the 75's placed first one and then a succession of curtains of shrapnel fire which steadily advanced right through the village and which spread right across it.

Germans came tumbling out of trenches in front of us and running back – at least some ran back, others remained where they fell. We then grumped rifle fire into them too and they got a very hot time of it. I believe there were about 3,000 of them in the village and they lost nearly 1,000 in killed and wounded before the French had finished with them.

When the fire from the 75's had ceased the French Infantry advanced and some came over to where we were and I thought they were going to 'coupe me gorge,' but I was able to reassure them that we were English before any accident of that sort occurred. We stood up and I was then able to collect my wounded and bury my dead (total casualties 4 killed and 7 wounded). When I had completed this job we returned to the battalion which we found in the market place at Aubers.

We stayed there till it was dark (about 2 hours) and then marched to billets for which we were grateful. Aubers was the first town I had been in after Germans had inhabited it for a short time. The whole place was strewn with pieces of furniture (mattresses, chairs, wardrobes, etc.) and the filth was indescribable. Outside the church was a crucifix with a figure of Christ upon it and here and there where piles of broken and empty bottles and more filth, while the crucifix was stained with what looked like ink and wine. It was altogether a revolting sight.

18th October – 12th November

Allies hold out in Ypres but at the virtual destruction of original BEF.

Tudor St John

Next morning after a good sound sleep and a nice hot breakfast we marched off to the sound of enemy guns in the near distance. We went for about 2 to 3 miles to a village called Herlier. As we approached the village we found several dead Scotsmen lying on the road and as we reached the outskirts we were greeted with a heavy shell fire which luckily was a bit over and all the shells burst 30 to 50 yards beyond us.

Had the range been accurate we should have got it badly as we were marching in column of fours across the front at the time. We took up our position in the rear of the village in reserve and there we sat all day doing nothing.

All this time we had been under the impression that the army were doing something in the way of a victorious advance and rather wondered why we were checked now. As the day wore on it became evident that quite a considerable battle was going on in front of us though we still thought it was the Germans' rear guard putting up a stiff resistance to our advance.

As dusk began to fall we were told that the regiment on the right of the brigade were going to take at the point of the bayonet, the road which the Germans were holding, and that we were to support their advance. Whether or not they ever got near their objective I don't know but the attack had failed before we could get near the place, and so we returned to the shelter of a heap of slag just in the village.

By this time it was dark and it was evident that we had raised a hornet's nest. The village was becoming an inferno of bursting shell and we clung very tightly to our slagheap. The noise of the battle and the light from the shells bursting in the dark gave the scene a very Dantesque impression. Just by the slagheap were two tall solitary fir trees and as each shell burst these were vividly outlined. The crash of the bullets on the far side of the heap and on the roofs of the houses was like the noise of a sudden crack across a sheet of ice. My company was soon the only one left at the heap, all the others having gone off to support some point or other. My orders were to keep in touch with the Seventh (Royal Fusiliers) and support them if necessary but I was not called upon to do so. At about 9.00pm I went forward and was shown a line along which my company were to be extended. For some reason or another a different company was to begin digging the trenches under my orders and my company were to relieve them in two hours.

I gave the officer in charge careful instruction about the type of trench I wanted dug and their position and returned to my own company who I got issued with all the spare ammunition I could raise which gave every man an extra 150 to 200 rounds. I also got water bottles filled and at the appointed hour marched down to our position. By this time the battle had died down and the silence was only interrupted by spasmodic bursts of rifle fire though a searchlight was being played on our lines and the place was occasionally lit up with flares and star shell. When I got down to our lines I found that the other people had started to dig quite the wrong type of trench and one which was of no use against shell fire and which we had to fill in again so that some three precious hours had been wasted.

Fortunately, as they had been digging for someone else's benefit they had not killed themselves by hard work so that the damage done was less than it might have been. I got my own men to work as soon as I could but I could not induce some of them to put any go into their digging. I tried to impress upon them that their lives depended on their efforts but they did not believe me and only worked hard when I or one of my subordinates drove them. As we could not be driving everyone at once, it began to get light before I was satisfied with the work done. I took care to give the lazy ones their own bits of trench to live in and as dawn was breaking we all got under cover and stood to arms.

19th October

B.E.F. transfer from Aisne to Flanders completed.

Tudor St John

No sooner had daylight fairly broken than we realised we were fairly in for it, shells came all around us, over us and before us. We all lay very low but the poor devils that had not dug deep when they had their chance had a bad time of it. One complete section of trench was wiped out and every man in it killed while a good many around were wounded. All of them got well frightened and we were thankful when they turned their attention elsewhere. They made no infantry attack where my company were but I could watch them deploying for attack on our left. I managed to get a message to this effect back to the gunner who put a few shrapnel among them and I was able to see a lot of them lying where they fell. We lay there all day and at night I had no difficulty in inducing the men to work hard at improving our position so far as was possible with the tools we had at our disposal.

20th October

Battle around Arras continues. Fierce German attack repulsed.

Tudor St John

Next day and the day after were spent much in the same way. We had a very open field of fire in front of us, which was the reason I imagine of our immunity from attack. The troops on our right and our left were being pretty heavily pressed all the time but except for being occasionally subjected to spells of shellfire from an uncomfortable oblique angle on our left, we were not threatened and our days were really almost dull.

On the night of the 20th there were several attacks on our flanks but again no one troubled us. We used the darkness to fill up with water, provisions and ammunition and to generally repair and improve our trenches.

21st October

Tudor St John

On the night of the 21st I received orders that all tools and extra ammunition were to be handed over to the transport and that we were to retire to a new position about a mile behind. This was to allow us to straighten up our line with the French who had left us occupying a dangerous salient.

H M Wilson
HMS Euryalus

Dear Mother,

We shall probably get into Plymouth today. Of course a good deal has occurred since you last heard from me. After the Admiral left we went down to Portsmouth on Wednesday morning (7th) where we coaled and left Friday evening and picked up our transports in the Channel at daylight on Saturday. There were 11 troop ships. About 10,000 territorials in all. They were going to India or Egypt. We went out to Gibraltar quite slowly. They are an awful nuisance as they never keep station properly and haven't got any signalmen on board. It was very calm going out and we got to Gibraltar on Wednesday. There was a French cruiser doing guard ships and a lot of German prizes. I saw some German prisoners who didn't seem very upset. The defence came in late in the evening. We swapped captains and navigators which was very sickening as we came off worst. We left the Bacchante at Gibraltar. I didn't write from there as we are bringing our own mails back as there is no overland service. We have had it extraordinarily calm. The transports are going onto Liverpool. I suppose we shall go out to Gibraltar again. I don't know if I told you we all said goodbye to the Admiral. He said he thought we should probably do this till Christmas. I do hope we shall commission another ship soon. Something with some real fighting value. I hope everything is all right at home.

Your loving son,

Hubert

22nd October

Germans capture Langemarck. Ten-day effort by Germans to break through allies' front line.

Tudor St John

The retirement was to be carried out from the left by companies and my company being the right flank company of the Battalion was not to move until the Battalion had all moved and was in its turn to be supported by the Lincolnshire Regiment who were on our right. The whole movement being timed to be completed about an hour before dawn began to break.

The enemy that night were very persistent with their attacks, particularly on our left, and it was partly on this account that the regiment on the extreme left were late in starting. Other reasons also contributed to the delay and the consequence was that half hour before day light we had not budged.

A major of the Lincolnshire Regiment came up to me very excitedly and asked why we were not gone and said that his Regiment had to wait for me before they could go. Of course I could give him no information but could only tell him that I could not go till Booth's company had gone and that he apparently was hung up in his turn by the other regiment.

The Major then suggested that I should go on my own account and not wait to be scuppered by daylight to which I replied that he could do as he liked but I was going to see my other company off first. That if any scuppering was to be done, the more of us there were to resist it, the worse for the Huns.

At the same time I did not at all like the delay. I got my men out of the trenches and lined up along the road all ready to move and then went and bustled Booth whom I found just preparing to shift having heard that the other people were falling in. I got him started and he went through my company who fell in behind and we bustled along at a fine pace just as dawn was breaking.

We did not get far before we found the road blocked by the Lincolnshire Regiment who were apparently not waiting to be scuppered, so I turned off and made my way across country to the battalion rendezvous which we reached in safety.

As a matter of fact the Germans never saw us go and did not wake up for a couple of hours after we had departed. They wasted about three hours heavily shelling the trenches we had vacated and finally launched an attack on them, which suffered heavily from our gunfire.

I now looked forward to a rest in nice billets and was told that this was to be our position. In those days the trench warfare, then in vogue, was a very different affair to the trench warfare of the present day (a year later).

We had no reserves and only an apology of a support. There was one battalion in each division, which was occasionally taken from the trenches and called a divisional reserve while it was supposed to be taking a rest. The result of this was that we only had one line of trenches which were more or less hastily contrived affairs, undrained and without dugouts.

We tried to make dugouts once but being unable to procure any material for supporting the roofs, they usually fell in the first time a shell bumped anywhere near them and buried the occupants. The habit was therefore discontinued by order of Divisional Headquarters.

One's turn of duty in the trenches was therefore not a comfortable period though personally I preferred it to our periods of so called rest; but to return to the story. We marched away to billets where we got breakfast (hot) and a mail or two and we were just settling down after our meal and a wash when we received orders to fall in at once. We were sent off to support the 8th Brigade which was in trouble at a place some 3 miles away.

When we got there we found that the pressure had been relieved and we were not wanted for the moment. We stuck there in a wood for the rest of the day and at nightfall returned to our billets, which we found had in the meantime been taken over by some sappers. We trudged away again and at last got into some very inferior billets in empty cottages which had no convenience for cooking the nice hot dinner for which we yearned.

Here we were allowed to stay for three hours and at midnight or thereabout we again paraded and two companies, of which mine was one, went off to dig some trenches under the guidance of an RE officer somewhere in the rear. I got to the place all right and eventually found the RE officer who took me round the trenches and explained to me how beautifully planned they were. This took him so long that by the time he was finished it was time for us to fall in again and join the rest of the battalion leaving a host of civilians, mostly refugees, to dig the trenches. I collected the battalion tools which I had had laid out ready for instant use and also those of the Brigade Headquarters.

23rd October

Battle of Ypres and continued heavy attacks near Langemarck.

Tudor St John

We reached our new billets at Rue de Barqueret at dawn and my company was told off to a farmhouse where we got plenty of hot food and water to wash in.

We spent quite a pleasant morning with mails and general cleaning up but after lunch we were sent out to dig trenches to be occupied in case of shellfire coming upon us. We were hardly out of the house before a 'crump' landed right in the middle of the farm buildings. We stayed out till dark and then returned to a farm for the night.

24th October

Belgium army flood low-lying coastal plain to prevent German advance. Indian troops arrive near Bethune.

Tudor St John

Next day we spent the morning and most of the afternoon in our funk holes but the Huns were apparently too busy to pay us much attention. I had a busy morning fixing up arrears of clerical work and organisation. Interior economy though important, does not get much attention during the kind of warfare that was being waged during those early months. In the middle of the afternoon we got orders to fall in and we proceeded to Rouge Croix where I took over billets in an abandoned cabaret.

It was dark when I took over but we got in somehow and I found a bed for the master to lie upon. We also managed to get some fuel for a dilapidated stove and got some hot soup. I had just lain down on my bed when I was 'wanted' at Headquarters. I got up and stumbled out into the rain and down to Headquarters, which was nearly half a mile away.

Here I was asked some minor questions or other which did not apply to me nor was I able to answer them. I got back to billets again and once more got turned in when once again I was roused and was told I was wanted. I had got half way to Headquarters when I met someone who told me to bring the Company along too.

I went back and got them fallen in and marched down to Headquarters. Here we stood for at least an hour when we were allowed to lie down in the wet grass by the roadside. The rain had stopped but there was a suspicion of frost and I was very cold.

25th October

Vermelles re-occupied by Germans.

Tudor St John

We stopped here till dawn and then were ordered to dig ourselves in, after which we were given a hot meal. The reason for the pleasant night's work was that the Germans had attacked the trench line and the Gordon Highlanders had broken and we were being held in readiness to support by counter attack if the Germans were not removed by other means. Fortunately they were so removed and we were left in peace for a few hours.

Somewhere about noon we were again fallen in and it was evident that excitement of some sort or another was going on. As soon as we had collected our men and fallen in I with the other company commanders was sent for and we were told the Germans had got through the brigade on our right and we were to make a counter attack in conjunction with the Royal Fusiliers.

We were to attack on the east of the Esterre – La Bassee road and my company was to lead the attack. I got them out in the required order and directed the platoon and section commanders. My instructions were hurried and rather muddled but I was told to do with them and not waste time so I set off, feeling anything but satisfied.

We had not got far before we came into contact with the 7th who seemed to be doing our job. I reported this and received an order to halt and close the company on the road as we were now to attack up the west side of the road. This reversion made us the rear company and I was ordered to be in battalion reserve.

We had progressed for about three quarters of a mile with our new attack when we heard that the 7th had done the work required and that we were to return to Rouge Croix. We did so and stopped there till dark. Here we saw quite a goodly number of German prisoners going back. I talked to one lot who looked very tired.

They had an officer with them who was really quite polite. There was also a boy of about 15 to whom I offered a biscuit. He refused it with scorn but one of the men took it and ate in with avidity. The boy showed a marvellous spirit and an apparently inexhaustible capacity for hate.

To my surprise I could not feel anything but pity for them although even in those days one had heard of the atrocities, which have since been made public. The Royal Fusiliers lost 12 officers in their attack so that it seemed a bit of luck for us that things were as muddled as they had been. So bad was the confusion on this occasion that the army corps commander came down to investigate this. The result, as I have since learned, that the divisional commander who had succeeded Hubert Hamilton was advised that he looked seedy and had better try a change of air in England.

As soon as it was dark we returned to our billets but I did not get much rest. It was the same thing again time after time, I was routed out to go and answer silly questions at Headquarters. At last I got an urgent summons and we were told that we were to relieve the Lincolnshire Regiment in the trenches, and were given careful instructions as to how we were to get there and how the relief was to be carried out.

26th October

Heavy fighting around Ypres.

Tudor St John

At midnight we fell in and marched down to our rendezvous at Croix Rouge. I formed up my Company as advanced guard along the road to Rue De Barquerot as according to orders. When the whole Battalion was fallen in I was told that we were to go via Pont Logie so I counter marched my advanced guard and formed them up along the La Bassee Road.

We got started off at last and reached our sector at about 3.00am Here we went into the farm where the Lincolnshire Battalion Headquarters was and were shown our trenches on the map and I was given a guide to take me down to mine. It was a wet night and the route lay over ploughed field and ditches, the latter being crossed by single slippery planks. I got to the trenches and found the officer in occupation feverishly awaiting my arrival afraid that I would not relieve him before daylight.

I took a hurried look round and remarked that the trenches were not very complete as such but was told by the officer that they had only been in them for three days, (which I knew), that they had taken them over from the staff, and that his men had been too tired to work at them!! Although they had not been very much harried.

I went back to the rendezvous to find that my company had been moved by some silly ass who had not left word as to where they had gone. I spent half an hour looking for them in the dark and at last found them mostly asleep in a ditch.

As there was not room for all of them in the trenches I left half a platoon behind with Battalion Headquarters and took the rest by slow, slippery and at times, sticky stages to my trenches where I found the officer nearly frantic with anxiety. However I got him and his men away in time and my own into their places but the margin was not a large one and we barely had time to settle down before we were standing to arms to greet the dawn.

As soon as it was light I had a good look round and came to the conclusion that there were no Germans nearer to us than 500 to 100 yards. I located our flank trenches and made a minute inspection of my own with a view to telling off working parties to improve them. I then had breakfast with a welcome tot of rum and posted look out men and then decreed a general doss till noon.

I had planned to begin work on improving the cover after the men had had dinner at midday but here I reckoned without my host who, on this occasion, was represented by the enemy who spent almost the entire afternoon in throwing shells at us. It began with the usual appearance of a Taube, which hovered over us and dropped its string of glittering balls. One gets to dread the Taubes as a field mouse must dread the hawk, only the Taube doesn't swoop and pounce (from choice that is to say) but instead drops its string of glass balls onto which the German gunners range.

Fortunately, on this occasion, either the Taube was not correctly over us or the range takers were inaccurate with the result that most of the shells went over us but they gave us a heavy bombardment and we suffered some casualties; also it prevented us from doing much useful work.

When darkness fell the shelling ceased and we started in. I put out two listening patrols calling for volunteers for this work, which in those days was somewhat of a novelty in soldiering. I could not get a single man to volunteer so ordered a man from each platoon to report to me at once and these I handed over in pairs to two N.C.O's who drove them out over the parapet. They went in fear and trembling although in reality they were just as safe there as they would have been outside the parados over which men went backwards and forwards without any hesitation whatsoever.

I always had trouble with the listening patrols. The men were all undoubtedly jumpy and hated the job and were always continually coming in to report imaginary advances by the Germans. I gave orders that they were not to come in until they actually saw men advancing but they then imagined that they saw them and I had to go out and show them it was only their imagination. The only use I had from them was on the first night when they reported digging was going on about 200 yards to our front.

The Germans were very active all night and attacked on both our flanks but they did not touch us though we were kept standing to arms for most of the night which was well illuminated by star shell and search lights. As far as possible we went on working but as a matter of fact I myself feared an attack and kept the men at their posts for a long time. I would not allow them to fire their rifles aimlessly as many men did and I found that by not doing so we were not fired at in return, a fact of which I made use of on succeeding nights to improve our trenches.

27th October

Neuve Chapelle taken by Germans.

Tudor St John

When daylight came we found the enemy entrenched at 300 to 100 yards away from us, a most unpleasant surprise for me. However at first their trenches were none too good and on both that morning and the morning after I bagged two Huns in the early hours making a total of four to my own (or rather my Sergeant Major's) rifle.

We were in the trenches till the night of October 29th, a total of four days and 5 nights during which we had a pretty lively time of it. In the first place we were heavily sniped at all the time and we lost a lot of men that way. I myself had a narrow shave. I went up to look at the head cover of a traverse which was reported as being dangerous.

No sooner had I stuck my head up than I got a bullet through the wrap I wore around my neck. It made a furrow in my beard but otherwise did no damage. The trenches were still bad and moving along them was a difficult matter and occasionally necessitated treading on dead men, as to throw the body over the parados only drew fire.

Thinking of this now and writing it down may appear to be merely bravado on my part. I mention it to show, what impressed me greatly at the time, how little one feared death in any form or thought of it when one was always face to face with it. One knew that one was certain to get a bullet in the course of time and that it might come along during the next few minutes.

It was during these days that Gordon fought so gallantly. His company was in our right flank trenches and the trenches again on his right were held by another Brigade. The Regiment in the trenches on his right gave way before a German attack and the Germans got right through behind us and charged Gordon from front and rear.

Having captured a field gun, Gordon got his men out of his trenches and charged three times and eventually drove the Germans off. They had to abandon the gun too but they got some straw and lit a fire under the limber containing the cordite, etc. This fire was seized by one of our Corporals who carried it out into the open and so saved the explosion and the gun though he himself was killed. In that fight Gordon lost all of his officers and most of his men but we still held the trenches.

During those days we were not blessed with fine weather. A lot of rain fell and the trenches became very sodden though it remained fairly warm. My officers then consisted of Everard Lamb (2nd captain) and two boys from the O.T.C. one of whom was called Thompson and I cannot remember the name of the other.

My pal Nunnely was transferred to Gordan's company after Herlies and was killed during Gordon's fight at Neuve Chapelle.

28th October

Neuve Chapelle re-taken by British.

29th October

Turkey enters war as an ally of the Central Powers.

Tudor St John

On Thursday evening, the 29th I got orders that we were to be relieved at 4.00pm and go into billets. I went down to Headquarters to report and meet the Officer who was to take over at about midnight. On the way there I was pretty heavily fired upon by one unknown man who seemed to follow me up, though he never hit me. I found Headquarters, which had been moved since I last saw them and took over my orders for relief and the officer who was to relieve me. He was an Indian army man and we were being relieved by a battalion of Ghurkas.

I got him and his orderly down to the trenches in safety and en route selected a good spot on the road for my company to assemble when they left. As we got in the Huns began a night attack, which lasted all the time I was showing the other man around. It then slackened for a bit and he got away but they kept pretty hard at it all night.

At about 4.00am our relief came along headed by an Englishman who was followed by a crowd of little boys. The Ghurka is only about 4 foot nothing in his socks and on this occasion, I learnt afterwards, his small stature combined with bad staff work was his undoing for no sooner had we left than the Germans attacked and the poor little men being too small to see over the parapet were scuppered and 400 of them were killed. We were not warned till too late that we were to be relieved by Ghurkas or told to build up a firing platform for them. This incident is a good one to show what a danger a staff officer is who neglects the smallest detail. The orders I gave for carrying out the relief were as follows. The Ghurkas were to line up behind the parados while our men were to leave with their N.C.Os. They were to proceed along a certain hedge, through a gate into a grass field, up behind another hedgerow, through another gap and through the corner of a turnip field into the road at a point where it was banked up. Here they were to form up behind the embankment and wait for me.

All went well so far as I could see and I got the Ghurkas into the trenches without any delay. Just as I started out a heavy attack on out right began to develop but only high shots were coming my way. These did not bother me and I made my way to the rendezvous to find no one there. I asked some gunners who were serving a howitzer in the turnip field if they had seen my men but they reported not.

So back I went again and found them all lying flat in the turnip field lower down, having taken cover there when the shots began to come over. I kicked them out of it and on to the road where I formed them up and told them what I thought of them, which done we went on to the Headquarters.

Robert Williams

Letter to his brother Alfred.

Dear Didden,

I am off for one day in London. Father and mother are up to see me, which is very good of them and very nice for me. The reason for my getting home is to take back the new car. I have been given another one for use in France, she is a beautiful great new Rolls Royce, and should be a great change to drive after the other one which really was too old for the work it was doing. I expect you are having an interesting time, although fighting does not come your way.

As for myself I return to France on Sunday and should be at my former work after a two hour run. I as you know I drive General Woodhouse who commands the entire medical branch in France. Although I see no fighting yet I cover great distances and see all that is going on from just behind the fighting to the bases.

You will be asking when is the war going to end; well I will tell you – no man knows!!! And father and I have just agreed that the problem of how long it will last after this winter is far too big to discuss. The general impression at the Front was that it could not be a very short war. Well I do not know of much news. I'll probably go to Dieppe and certainly make for Aberville, which is now our base to work from.

Your affectionate brother,

R Williams

30th October

Ypres closely pressed by Germans.

Tudor St John

Here we waited for about half an hour or more till the other companies who had experienced some difficulty in getting away, joined up with us when we all proceeded down the road to Rouge Croix which we reached as daylight appeared. We went to Ville Chapelle which was where I had joined the battalion on October 14th and got into billets there and had breakfast.

We had been fighting continuously now since the 13th October and were all absolutely tired out. The Brigade had lost 54 officers and 12,000 men during this period and we hoped for our long promised rest. We stopped all that day in Ville Chapelle as the general who was to take over our sector had not arrived and also things were not going too well with the Indians who had relieved us and who were having a bad time of it.

At about 3.00pm we fell in and eventually marched off to Esterre to our billets outside that town, when we were told that we were to have a weeks rest and refit. I had billets in a nice farmhouse where the inmates insisted on turning out of their beds and sitting up all night to allow the officers beds to sleep in. I turned into a soft bed with snowy white sheets and was soon asleep only to be woken up somewhere about 10.00pm with orders to the effect that the battalion would rendezvous at the cross roads at 5.45am The news rather disturbed my nights sleep as to begin with I had reached that state of weariness when sleep will not come to one.

31st October

HMS Hermes sunk.

Tudor St John

We turned out at about 4.30am and got breakfast. I also got a bit of a wash in a bucket. I found the men quite cheerful being under the impression that they were going further back as our billets were wanted for someone else. I didn't disabuse their minds and got them to the rendezvous in good time, everyone else was late as the hour of starting had been put forward at the last moment.

I ascertained that we were going for a 15-mile march to support the Cavalry Brigade who were holding the line south of Ypres and who were being hard pressed. We pressed on and got to a place called Neuve Eglise where my company were told off to dig trenches which was bad luck on them as they were the only company which had not been given a day and night as support at Neuve Chapelle.

However they were wonderfully cheerful and we had some new blood in too in the shape of reinforcements who had joined us after we had come out of the trenches. These had arrived under Bob Fletcher and Robin Willans, neither of whom lived to see a week of fighting. After we had been digging for about three hours they gave up the idea of entrenching there and we sat about on the roadside till dark when we went into billets at Kemmel, with orders to be prepared to turn out at a moments notice. I was very careful to carry out this order and saw that every N.C.O. knew exactly where his men were to fall in. It required some care as the billets were in a mill and the men had to climb down staircases and ladders from the lofts. My care bore fruit too for we were as usual the first company ready and were ready sometime before the other companies that should have proceeded us according to the order of march. The result was that I got a damning for waiting for the other companies and we were sent into the foreground of the battle out of our turn but that is another story.

1st November

Battle of Ypres continues. Germans capture Messines, Hollebeke and Wytschaete. HMS Monmouth and Good Hope sunk.

H M Wilson
Bedford Hotel
Tavistock

Dear Mother,

Thanks very much for the letters and the pheasant etc. They arrived all right as a torpedo boat brought our mails off last Tuesday. We came into Plymouth yesterday as we had three cases of enteric from eating oysters. We are now the flagship of R. A. Wemyss. We are in command of the patrol in the mouth of the Channel. They gave us a day's leave while we were coaling, so I hired a motor bike and sidecar. We are having lunch here. It is fairly respectable. Thanks very much for the links. I am sorry I did not thank you for them before. We got a signal a few nights ago saying, 'Commence hostilities at once against Turkey.' I wish we were back in the North Sea with Christian. There is a tale that he is to have a court martial, which would be bad luck indeed. They say he ought to have been there on the spot. Bad luck about the Hermes being sunk. I wonder when we shall loose a dreadnought. I don't think one needs worry about the German howitzers. They would never hit a ship. Naval gunnery is different to land shooting.

Your loving son,

Hubert

Tudor St John

At 2.00am we got the order to fall in. I had slept on a heap of straw in a pub and had slept very soundly too. The men were very smart at falling in and we were soon ready and waiting to take up our place in the line of march. After waiting for quarter of an hour I was hauled over the coals for not going on as soon as we were ready as the matter in hand was very urgent. No one had thought it worth while to tell me anything about urgency but I had given up arguing or even feeling aggrieved about these things as orders and counter-orders came with such frequency that it was difficult to carry on at all let alone to do the right thing.

We marched off and halted again at some point on the Kemmel – Wytschaete Road. Here was a limber on fire and every now and again a cartridge would blow up. The sky was lit all around by fires and there was a noise of continual musketry intermingled with the deeper note of field guns.

I dozed for about half an hour with my body in a wet ditch and my head pillowed on a turnip. Turnips make bad material for pillows and I woke feeling cold and stiff with rather a head on me, to be told to go to the head of the battalion at once. I went and was ordered to take my company and Bob Fletcher's and to support the Lincoln Regiment in their attack on Wytschaete.

I could get no information about the strength of the enemy or the exact position of the Lincolns. All I was told was that the latter were on the right of the road and had started an hour before. The country between the village and me, I was also told, was open, which was a lie as it was very enclosed, chiefly by barbed wire. Finally, that we would come under artillery fire almost at once and that I was to hurry up and do what I could to support the attack.

I decided that the best thing to do was to pretend to develop a strong attack on the left or north side of the road and with this object in view we set off in lines of platoons across country in the dark.

We soon got hung up in barbed wire and I found that only one of the four cutters, that were considered a sufficient issue to a company of infantry by the General Staff, was left. The three others had been borne by men who had become casualties of some kind or another. I also had my own private pair and so we got along somehow, but it took us until dawn to get within 1000 yards of the village. Here I called a halt and went to find Fletcher. Him I found digging a hole in the ground and murmuring something about it being his baptism of fire.

I told him to keep close to the road so that I could find him if I wanted him and went off to the left again to push my company on into a wood which ran apparently right up to the village and round to the north of it. I found a young subaltern of the lifeguards in the wood with a few men and suggested that he push on and clear the wood if he could do so.

He said he wanted his breakfast and did not know much how to soldier off a horse but would do his best. I also detailed a platoon to assist him and went on to find the two platoons in the firing line.

I had sent Everard Lamb up in charge of these two platoons in the dark as both of them were commanded by young and inexperienced men and I had been afraid that they would loose touch with everyone in the dark. I now intended to send Lamb back to the support and to direct the platoons where to go and what to do and then to rejoin him. As a matter of fact I never found him and never saw him again as he was killed that day. We had lived together for a fortnight and I had come to be very fond of him.

When I got up near the village I found one platoon digging themselves in about 100 yards away from the village. I walked out of the wood and up to them and told the sergeant in charge to push on as there was heavy firing going on our right where the Lincolnshire Regiment where.

I then walked back to the wood to try and get hold of Lamb but no one knew where he was. I then came back to the edge of the wood and found that the other platoon had advanced about 20 yards and were lying down and digging head cover. I walked out to them and found everyone very jumpy and fed up with things generally and particularly at the absence of breakfast. I told them to lie where they were till I found out where everyone else was and then to go on into the village when I whistled them to do so.

I next went to the road to try and get hold of Fletcher and to find out how things were going. I found Roderick with a few men and some wounded behind a cottage at the edge of the road. One of the wounded had a broken thigh and was kicking up an almighty shindy so I tried to get hold of stretcher from the Lincolns across the road. Apparently the road was commanded by machine guns in the village and no one could cross it. I tried to find out where Fletcher was but no one knew.

The Lincolns reported by shouting that they were having a bad time of it. I waited there for a few minutes hoping that Fletcher would come along so that we could settle on some kind of action.

While there someone reported that firing was coming from the wood. I asked Roderick to send a man over to find out what it was but he did not jump at the idea and as it was my company who were supposed to be going through the wood I said I would go myself and return again to find Fletcher. I also could not make out where my other platoon had got to and this I was anxious to know.

I had just come across a ploughed field, which was about 200 yards wide and had not been alarmed by any close bullets so I walked quietly out from behind the cover of the cottage and proceeded towards the wood. I had not gone very far however when I became the centre of attraction of a hot fire which must I think have come from a machine gun.

I started to run to the wood at once and the ground all around me was spattered up like the surface of a puddle in a rainstorm. I got another 30 or 40 yards when I felt as if I'd suddenly hit my right arm against a hard obstacle in the dark. It was a very hard and very sharp blow and left a numb sort of tingling sensation in my arm. It was quite different from the stinging of the blows of one or two pebbles which had been knocked into my legs by the shots on the ground, which had hurt me quite as much.

I still ran on but the wood looked a long way off and the shock of the wound had scared me a bit. I felt rather dizzy and out of breath (I was running with a coat and all my equipment on me) so I decided I would do a die and selecting as comfortable place as I could I wheeled round the most approved Caton Woodville fashion and fell on my face.

This had the desired effect for a minute or two and the firing stopped. I gave them time to turn their attention elsewhere and then proceeded to get myself more comfortable with a view to examining the damage to my arm and of tying it up. I must have wriggled too much, however, for again a hot fire was opened on me. I lay for a few seconds wondering where it would get me; the bullets splashing mud all round me.

Suddenly I felt as if someone had gently drawn something rather hot along my shoulder and round my throat. This could not have been the bullet as it appeared to me to take quite an appreciable time to get from my left shoulder to the right side of my throat. I think it must have been the blood flowing. Certainly as soon as it reached my throat I began to cough blood through my mouth and nose and felt as if I was choking and everything looked a sort of blue colour.

I thought I was done for and wondered how my family would take the news and whether I would know how they took it. I felt aggrieved and angry at the thought of leaving this jolly old world for to me it had always been a jolly place and it seemed hard lines having to leave it without seeing Roger and Madge again. However, I prayed to God to hurry the matter up as I was getting very uncomfortable.

How long all this took I don't know but one moment I thought I was gone and the next as it seemed to me I felt as if I was up and away in the high Alps somewhere breathing breath after breath of invigorating air. This must have been caused by the cessation of the bleeding which enabled me to breath not only though the nose and mouth but also through both the wounds in my neck.

I lay there for I suppose about 5 hours. It was very cold and the ground was wet and I remember having fits of shivering either from cold or funk or both. I could not see what was going on in the way of fighting but once they searched the field I was in with shrapnel. It was a narrow sort of field bounded on one side by the wood and on the other by the road and the width of curtain presumably fired by four guns seemed to my eyes to cover the field most effectively. I watched two salvoes burst in front of me and then thought I would surely get my quietus but the third effort went over me and all was well once again.

I could not use my right arm at all but I could wave my legs about in the air and also manipulate my walking stick with my left hand. When I had been there an hour or two I saw some gunners at the edge of the wood. I waved both stick and legs at them and they stopped and conferred about me but would not risk coming into the open to see what I wanted. My heart sank as I watched them go away.

Help eventually reached me through one of my own sergeants who came along. He gave me water and then went off for stretcher-bearers who arrived with a doctor about half an hour later. My, I was glad to see them!!! They cut off all my equipment and got me onto the stretcher and carried me to the dressing station, which was about 2 miles away so far as I could judge. From the lurid language of the stretcher-bearers it might well have been ten miles and I might have been a tonne of coals they were carrying. However we got there and my wounds were dressed with iodine which hurt horribly. I was given some morphia that had no effect on me, and put into an ambulance, which I think belonged to an Indian contingent, and taken joltingly to Kemmel where I was laid in a chapel and had more iodine applied.

I lay there till about 5.00pm when I was removed by motor ambulance to Bailleul. It was an appalling journey for me. There were four slightly wounded Tommies in the ambulance, which was closed up, and all the Tommies smoked woodbines all the time and our way lay over a much damaged Route Pave. Every jolt gave me 'gyp' and I was nearly suffocated and unable to speak. Every time I tried to speak the air blew out of my wounds instead of going through my larynx. By the time I reached the hospital at Bailleul I was pretty nearly done. I must have seemed hopeless for they did not take the trouble to transfer me from the stretcher to bed and I spent a sleepless night. I found one of my subalterns was there too with a broken wrist.

2nd November

Germans prepare for attack on Ypres. British lines broken at Nerve Chapelle, and Germans re-occupy.

W H Carver

Uniforms and leather equipment arrived in stages in early November prior to the battalion's move to Hornsea on the East Coast. Ankle deep mud and uncompleted huts were awaiting the men. The first few meals had to be cooked in the new latrine buckets. Like many Battalions they had a few rifles and even fewer rounds to use and this was strictly against the enemy. This concerned Richardson who wrote to the War Office. They replied by wanting to know the efficiency of the rifles to which Richardson replied... 'Rifles will certainly go off, doubtful which end.'

Notes taken from The Trench, *page 31.*

Tudor St John

Next morning I was put on board an ambulance train and sent to Boulogne. I do not remember much about the journey except that I occupied one side of a first class carriage and a man with a disabled limb occupied the other, oddly I met this man six months later.

I must have been pretty bad because I remember that the R.A.M.C. orderly who was looking after us thought it safe enough to go through my pockets and relieve me of £10 or £12 in gold and a few odds and ends as well. I tried to call the medical officer's attention to this when I got to Boulogne but I could not make myself heard. A strong feeling of furious indignation no doubt helped to increase my exhaustion, at any rate when I was eventually put to bed in No.11 General Hospital at the Imperial Hotel at Boulogne I was past knowing much about anything and how I got through that night I cannot remember. At Boulogne I was put into a ward with four other beds all full. Three of the others died before my eyes and the fourth was sent to England and died a few days after he arrived there. My life was saved chiefly by the devotion of Nurse Binns who spared herself no labour or fatigue to do all in her power to give me ease.

One incident in my illness I must record chiefly on account of its weird unpleasantness happened shortly after I got to Boulogne and before the wounds had healed much. It was at night and I must have coughed very hard or something, at any rate, the effect was that the air came through the wound and was forced up under my skin so that my face was blown up like an air balloon. I was terribly frightened and sent for the night surgeon who gave me an injection of something – I think Digitalis, which calmed things down for me. At first too I used to dream horrible dreams always the same that I was turned out and sent back to the trenches and couldn't find my company, but the awakening to reality in a nice safe hospital was distinctly good.

About a fortnight after I got to Boulogne I developed Sceptic Pneumonia. Had I got it 48 hours sooner nothing could have saved me. As it was, the skill of my doctors, who then were, Sir Francis Makin, Sir John Rose Bradford and Mr Meares and Mr Warr, the house surgeons, combined with the splendid nursing of Nurse Binns and Sister Howe got me through it. They also got me through an attack of bronchitis that came on top of it.

4th November

Battle of Ypres continues.

5th November

Britain declares war on Turkey.

Canon Andrews

Finding it difficult to obtain a passage to England, I decided to join up as a stretcher-bearer with the Australians. The departure of the troops was an unforgettable site. Australians referred to England as home so the whole of Sydney came out to send us on our way and bid us 'God speed'. I got on board as soon as possible and found myself a bunk where I could lie low and be as inconspicuous as possible. The Australians came on singing and at last we were off! Eventually all was quiet and so it seemed sleep was finally on the cards. But from a hammock above an alcoholic voice was suddenly heard shouting to his chum 'I say Nobby have you heard the latest? We've got a bloody parson in our lot, so mind your language.'

Immediately heads popped out from hammocks everywhere. 'A parson!' they shouted demanding details of this depressing news. After a heated debate a voice was heard to say 'Well, what about it? He can't help it poor devil!' and there was peace once more.

Notes from Canon's Folly, *page 51.*

9th November

Ypres under violent German attack. British position again in danger.

10th November

H M Wilson
HMS Euryalus

Dear Mother,

It is very sad about Jackie Charlton. The Monmouth is a sister ship to the Cumberland. I knew a good many snotties on her and the Good Hope. The people on the Monmouth were only second term at Dartmouth. We intercepted a lot of wireless signals about that thing on the East Coast. I believe there are a lot of pictures of the Euryalus with something about Heligoland to be had. I will try and get hold of some.

Your loving son,

Hubert

11th November

British trenches taken near Ypres, then recovered. HMS Niger sunk.

Canon Andrews

During my first few days aboard I was sleeping with the men who fed the horses so I helped them and ate with them. We were a happy crowd and I was sorry to leave them when the doctor asked for me to assist him instead. The voyage was enjoyable, though we seemed to go very slowly. We had to sail inside the Great Barrier Reef due to a German cruiser escaping from the watchful eye of the navy. Then we found out it was somewhere in the Indian Ocean playing havoc with our shipping.

Notes taken from Canon's Folly, *page* 52.

17th November

End of 1st Battle of Ypres. Stationary warfare. Lloyd George introduces his first war budget.

W H Carver

An invasion 'scare' sends the Hull Pals to Hornsea, much earlier than intended because the huts are not all completed when they arrive. For the next 6 months they were based here.

Notes taken from The Trench, *page 30.*

22nd November

Trench warfare established along entire Front.

28th November

Turkish advance towards Suez.

29th November

King leaves England to visit army in France.

16th November

W H Carver

Great excitement when the troops heard for the first time the German naval bombardment of the east coast towns of Scarborough, Whitby and Hartlepool. Three cruisers had opened fire suddenly, causing much damage and 1000 causalities.

Notes taken from The Trench, *page 31*

20th November

Tudor St John

I stayed in Boulogne till the 20th of December which was the first day that I was not too ill to be moved to a ship. The sea was flat enough to allow me to travel on it with a reasonable hope of not being sea sick. I have never been so important a person as I was on that voyage.

Unlike ordinary wounded heroes I was not herded onboard hours before the ship started but said goodbye to Miss Blakely, the matron and the nurses, and proceeded in a chair to the ship just before it was to sail. Nurse Binns came down to the ship with me and Sir Francis Makin and Sir John Rose Bradford were both waiting to see me onto the ship. Mr Meares was sent over with me all the way to Torquay to look after me.

21st December

First German air raid on Britain. British troops assist Indian Army to repel Germans at Givenchy.

Tudor St John

When we got to Southampton the next morning a Brigadier General was waiting for me and I was the first off the ship and taken into a special Torquay train which left within half an hour. We got to Torquay at about 7.00pm that night and here again I was the centre of attention. I was to go to Mrs Burns' hospital and Mrs Burns had got an idea that I could walk so had only brought a motor for me and no ambulance so that I had to wait amidst a curious crowd of onlookers while an ambulance was procured. When I got to Stoodley Knowle I was put into the drawing room until a room was got ready for me and I was there for quarter of an hour among a number of officers, one of whom was Dorman Smith, who had been one of my subalterns since March, but who did not recognise me until I spoke to him!!

25th December

Unofficial Christmas truce declared by soldiers along Western Front.

W H Carver

As 1914 drew to a close the rifle problem began to ease due to the Battalion raising money and buying their own ammunition. Today the men had their first experience of trying to get a bull's eye. Throughout December they had remained on coastal duty. This involved patrolling the shoreline and learning to dig trenches on the tops of cliffs.

Notes taken from The Trench.

28th December

Robert Williams

Dear Aunt Charlotte,

So sorry to hear you were feeling ill. I hope you are quite right now. You know father gave me a new Rolls car some two months back which goes beautifully so making my job much easier; but it is a strange life and I doubt you would recognise me when in this car.

Still all good things come to an end in time!! The war news seems better especially from the east, I think next autumn should see peace settled, let us only hope it will be lasting. Cold, rain and mud seem to be the weather on this side. With all best wishes to you all,

Your affectionate nephew,

R Williams

29th December

H M Wilson
HMS Euryalus

Dear Mother,

We get in this afternoon and I expect we will coal tomorrow and go out Thursday. I hope you have got my letters and postcards all right. We had rather a different Christmas Day as you may imagine. They doled out Christmas cards from the King and the Queen on Christmas morning. I expect we shall get our Princess Mary's sweets etc when we get our mails.

After church all the officers went and drank fizz in the wardroom. It was pretty indifferent. We didn't do badly as the Admiral sent us three bottles of port and a large cake and the Commander produced some chocolates. We have changed round now.

I attend the navigator and run the picket boat. It means getting up at 4am every other morning at sea. It is not a bad job. More interesting than engineering. We have all been hoping for action with one of the German light cruisers but I am afraid it is too late now. Did father get home for Christmas?

Your loving son,

Hubert

1915

⟜ 1st January ⊸

Allied offensive at Artois and Champagne. Institution of Military Cross. HMS Formidable sunk.

J F Williams

While steaming westward to exercises in the Channel, we heard reports that the Formidable had been sunk by a torpedo. The Fleet was in the act of turning 16 points when the signal came through. The course was then altered further to get out of the presumed area of danger. Two cruisers were left behind to assist if possible. The second torpedo hit the Formidable some time after the first but it is believed this was intended for the Diamond who was almost alongside at the time, the torpedo just missing her stern.

W H Carver

By the New Year training was stepping up as various specialists were created among them i.e. machine gunners and signaller's etc. Company Commanders were asked to recommend those NCOs capable of higher ranks while all those who had only been acting NCOs now had their rank confirmed. It was asserted that the qualifications to become a NCO demanded character, determination and good mental powers. This prevented employers and relations trying to pull strings. It was important that the 10th had the right attitude, for within months they expected to be heading for France. Route marches of between 15 and 20 miles were used to get the men to peak fitness.

Notes taken from The Trench, *page 31.*

Tudor St John

I had been led to believe that once in Devonshire I would soon get all right again and was disappointed to find that instead I was getting worse. In fact I had quite made up my mind that I was going to die and as I afterwards found out the doctors had similarly decided. However, my luck did not forsake me though it left matters pretty late.

When it did again come to my assistance it did so with a vengeance. Doctors Gillette and Green who were attending me had called in a laryngologist to consult but none of them had come to a definite diagnosis of my case. They decided therefore to call for Mr Hill who is a very good laryngologist in London. Mr Hill was unable to come at once but said he would come in a week if possible. It was decided therefore to move me to a nursing home in Torquay where Hill could see me more conveniently and I was to go on Thursday and he was to come on Saturday. Now I had quarrelled with a night nurse who had been got in to act as special for me and who was of some age and not very conversant with modern surgery, etc. and who, therefore, did not trouble herself much about me. Mrs Burns had sacked her and on Tuesday I got a new one whose name I forget as I called her 'Bo Peep' all the time. She was an A1 nurse, however and very good to me. To cut a long story short I was a lot worse on Wednesday night and Bo Peep went and woke up Mrs Burns. She woke up the house surgeon, Dr Ward, and two other nurses who all said I was in no danger though undoubtedly worse. Dr Gillette also agreed in this but remained at the hospital to look at me every half-hour.

In the meantime Mrs Burns had a cylinder of oxygen (which she had got into the hospital at the beginning against everyone's advice) moved into my room. After an hour or two Gillette became doubtful and sent for Dr Green who said at once that he must perform a tracheotomy immediately though he doubted it was too late. Meantime I was slowly dying of suffocation but thanks to the oxygen I was kept alive long enough for the injections of strychnine and ether to be given me and to take effect.

Dr Green operated without any anaesthetic and I nearly died on the table but was just able to cough in time and so got rid of a fine abscess as big as my two fists. Had I not changed my nurse, had Mrs Burns not insisted on watching me against the advice of her staff, had she not had the oxygen in the house also against advice I should have died that night. Moreover, had the climax postponed its arrival till next day I should have been moved and would have died for certainty on the journey. From now onwards I never looked back though once again my luck served me in a minor way. This was when after having sat upright for three months I developed a bad boil on my tail just when I was once again able to lie down.

6th January

J F Williams

From what news we have collected by various sources we know that the loss of life has been very heavy. In view of the fact the incident has turned out so serious not only in the heavy loss of life but also the loss of the ship, it might be of interest to try and remember what my ideas where concerning the reasons why we had come to sea and under what restrictions.

7th January

J F Williams

I have written nothing for the last three months. The reason is mostly laziness on my part. My excuse being the dull time that we have been having and the lack of interesting information. We eventually went back to Portland after the bulk of the BEF was over. We were never interfered with and looking back at what we did one realises what a chance they missed.

A very quiet time was had at Portland and was only interrupted by two or three days firing and two dashes up the channel (on the occasion of the Yarmouth raid) when we never got further east than Dungeness. We twice sent a couple of ships to Sheerness or Dover for the operations on the Belgium coast but unfortunately were never sent ourselves. We remained in Sheerness doing nothing but occasional landing parties until about Dec 14th when we went out to do some firing. While outside we heard of the Scarborough raid and although we stopped outside the bar until the last minute we got no orders to do anything and so had to go inside again. Life remained dull till just before lunch on Christmas day when we heard the sound of guns. The fog that had been surrounding us cleared just in time and I was the first to see a German aeroplane, which was just passing very high up.

There was a good deal of firing at it from the shore and our aeroplanes went up after it but we saw nothing more. Nothing further of interest occurred until it was decided we had all been in harbour long enough. I had been feeling this for some time hence the reason I have been applying to get a job as number one of a destroyer. As has so often been pointed out the more hours a ship stays in harbour the less efficient she becomes. We left for exercise in the channels right at the end of December.

10th January

Germans bomb Dunkirk.

Tudor St John

I stayed at Torquay till the middle of February during which time Nurse Wilkinson nursed me. I managed between January the 9th and February 14th to increase my weight from 7st 8lbs to 9 stone. On February the 14th I went up to London to King Edward VIIth Hospital for Officers where I stopped for many months. Here I was attended to by Sir St. Claire Thomson and Mr Hope and looked after by a number of nurses among whom Nurses Taylor, Hargreaves, Etheridge, Carr and Rowlett did the lion's share of taking care of me. And here I must also mention Sister Hopkinson whom I so constantly met in the operation theatre which I have now visited some 27 times and which I expect to visit on several other occasions.

19th–20th February

First German zeppelin attack on England.

4th February

British casualties to date are around 104,000.

Canon Andrews

On arrival in Egypt we joined up with the AIF who were encamped near the pyramids. Soon after we got news we were to embark for an unknown destination. We were told we were the advance party and were to march to Cairo and on no account should anyone fail to complete the march.

The agony of that march to Cairo is something I shall never forget. I had played football the day before and had never felt fitter but as soon as the march began I developed violent pains in my innards. The Australians seeing I was in trouble bit by bit took my equipment off me to carry themselves.

By the time we arrived in Cairo I was being supported by one of those burly diggers each side of me and they kept me marching to the end. We made for the bar where they gave me a brandy. This didn't help so they tried Crème de Menthe on me and this seemed to relieve the pain a little. All I can remember of that terrible night was these Australians leaning over me dosing me with Crème de Menthe until I was finally asleep in the corner.

Next morning we were put on a train to Alexandria and I slept like a log for the entire journey. I woke up at Alexandria feeling as fit as a fiddle and walked straight onto the transport ship. The only haggard looking fellows on parade were the chaps who had stayed up all night with me and had carried all my kit. I have treated Crème de Menthe with great respect ever since.

Several days later we sailed at sunset into Mudros Bay on Lemnos and there we saw something we would never see again. Combined fleets of French and British fighting ships with an unending line of transports packed with troops from every part of the empire. Fortunately not one of that enthusiastic force could look ahead as we waited week after week wondering what we were waiting for. Had we been allowed to attack the Gallipoli Peninsula immediately the whole campaign might have been a success.

Notes taken from Canon's Folly, *page* 54.

5th February

Lusitania arrives in Liverpool under an American flag.

7th February

American flag on the Lusitania justified for purpose of evading capture at sea. Turks officially stated to be in full retreat east of Suez Canal.

H M Wilson

Dear Mother,

We are off tomorrow evening and I don't suppose we shall be home for six months or so. I don't suppose you will hear from me too. We have had pouring rain all day and I have been away in the picket boat nearly all day and got well soaked.

Everyone is awfully glad to go abroad. There seems to be a lot going on in the East and we ought to get some excitement. We have just bought a new lot of gramophone records to keep us going while abroad. I will write as soon as possible.

Your loving son,

Hubert

19th February – August

Allied amphibious attack on Dardanelles and Gallipoli – initiated by Winston Churchill, who resigns as a consequence. Bombardment of forts at entrance to Dardanelles by British and French. Turks attack allied forces.

20th February

Germans gain ground at Ypres. Continued bombardment of Dardanelles.

22nd February

Germany announces pursuit of Russians now over.

23rd February

W H Carver

The Battalion marches 17 miles to Hull. Senior officers rode horses, as was customary. Food and drink were supplied to the men on arrival but some slipped away from the ranks on the homeward journey and made for the nearest station on the Hornsea Line!

Notes taken from The Trench.

27th February

Dardanelles operations hindered by bad weather.

5th March

In the Dardanelles, narrow forts are bombarded by Queen Elizabeth from Gulf of Saros. British warships bombard Smyrna.

C Carver
Royal Military Academy, Woolwich

My dear Prof.,

I am afraid it is quite inexcusable my not having written before so I will not waste time doing so. My own history since we last met has been as follows... I got mumps and then went up for the army exam on the 21st of September. Returned to Rugby for a month till I heard I had passed into Woolwich. I came up to the shop in October and here I am a Corporal with six weeks to go before we are commissioned. I am destined for the Royal Field Artillery and so far have enjoyed myself immensely. We hope to be at the Front any time between now and June; we little thought of this last summer term.

Your old time tutored,

Cadet Corporal C C Carver

H M Wilson
HMS Euryalus
Gulf of Smyrna

Dear Mother,

I suppose there has been something in the papers about our bombarding of Smyrna. We left Port Said in a hurry on Wednesday evening. We had a sort of Council of War and went into the gulf about 12 o'clock in line, ourselves leading. The idea is to destroy the fortifications and make it useless for a submarine base. The turret gun got about 4 hits out of 6 which is good for an old gun.

We then closed to 10,000 yards and continued firing. Two of their magazines blew up and then we steamed out about 6 miles and anchored. I got one or two photos of ships firing but I am not sure if they will come out. The difficulty is you never know when you've knocked out a battery, as they are very well concealed and often won't reply as this might give them away.

Your loving son

Hubert

Robert Williams

In the spring of 1915 Robert Williams returns to England and is given a commission into The Grenadier Guards.

12th March

French begin massing in North Africa for Dardanelles Campaign.

13th March

Heavy fighting around Ypres.

J F Williams

In order to get information back home and have his letters pass through the censors, John devised the following code for letters to his parents:

Dear Father...	No fresh news.
My Dear Father...	We have done nothing but things are looking bright.
No More...	Capture of German merchant vessels.
Your Loving Son...	Had a successful engagement and am alright.

Loving Son...	Mines are doing all the damage against us.
Yours...	Have had an engagement.
No space left...	Both sides are suffering heavily.
Must finish...	Things are looking bad.
No time left...	Our losses are being suppressed in the papers.
Your son...	Things ought to end soon.
No more now...	Am east of London.
Finish now...	Am North of Thurso.
Finish...	English losses (if underlined – heavy)
Must end...	German losses (if underlined – heavy)
No more time...	Hard times with not much result.
No more space...	Bright outlook for England.

2nd April

H M Wilson

My dear Mother,

We are rather expecting the Turks to attack the canal in force. I think we shall very likely go to the Dardanelles when they get nearly through. About 10,000 marines and Naval Division arrived here the other day.

They have come down from the Dardanelles where they aren't wanted just yet. There is really nothing doing here except to hope for the Turks to arrive.

Your loving son,

Hubert

8th April

H M Wilson

Dear Mother,

Thank you for your letters. We are going to another job now and shall get rid of this Admiral. I expect you might hear of us down at the Dardanelles or at Constantinople. I met the Williams who stood for Northwich. He is in the RND out here.

He knew father I think. I expect we shall have a pretty exciting time at the Dardanelles. We shall probably loose a good many ships and men, naval and military as they propose to go through at all costs. We are leaving this week

Your loving son,

Hubert

22nd April

Second Battle of Ypres continues to mid May; town mostly destroyed.

24th April

Alfred Williams

Extract from the log of Midshipman A. M. Williams, Gallipoli Gazette Autumn 1965.

Arrived at Tenedos at 6.40 am. There was a fresh breeze and the sea was choppy. There seemed some reason to doubt if a landing could be effected the next day but the sea went down through the night. Major General Hunter Weston, G.O.C. of the 29th Division came on board at noon with his staff.

In the afternoon the lifeboats were towed over from the Caledonia. At 7.00pm fleet-sweeper W4 came alongside and discharged the Lancashire Fusiliers on board. At 9.40 we proceeded very slowly with our picket-boats and steam pinnaces made fast astern, and four lifeboats astern of each of them. The remaining boats were towed by trawlers and fleet sweepers.

Canon Andrews

We were anchored with another ship in the crowded harbour and our man in charge was a Major Clogson who wore an eyeglass. This delighted the Australians, as they believed all English Majors wore them. He was a pretty smart officer, and as we were to learn, totally fearless.

His task had not been an easy one with discipline hard to control with men waiting on ships day after day. On the first Sunday after we had arrived I was asked to give the sermon and this job I continued to do while we waited. After so many days and weeks of waiting and preparation, at last we were told that we were to land on Gallipoli before it was light the following Sunday morning.

Ever since, as April draws to a close, a picture of that night before we landed flashes through my mind in vivid detail. A concert and a speech by an officer in command. He tells us we will be in for a hell of a time. The coast is a honeycomb of machine guns and there is barbed wire everywhere along the shore and into the sea and the Turks are waiting for us, and anyone who sees the sun set tomorrow will be a lucky man.

Then the scene changes and we transfer in the darkness from our transport to a destroyer. How we got there I still am not sure for we seemed to wait for hours in the darkness on deck. Then a naval officer comes to me and asks if I will take communion service.

It is quietly announced to be held at midnight. Men I have never seen before come up and whisper 'I haven't been confirmed, but may I come?' I reply, 'tell them, all can come if they want to, everybody.' I find I am giving orders now – that's funny, I am only a Private. Fortunately it is very dark so no one can see.

A young naval officer fetches a box and we convert it into an altar. The lump in my throat, as I dread the dawn, has disappeared. I watch the men crowding up into one end of the ship where I was told to hold the service. We wait in the darkness in silence before I start. Row upon row of men kneel about the deck so I can hardly reach them all; soldiers and sailors from all parts of the Empire. It is too dark for my tears to be seen as I whisper to each one 'preserve thy body and soul unto everlasting life.

Notes taken from Canon's Folly, *page* 55.

H M Wilson

840 men of the Lancashire Fusiliers arrived on board about 6pm Euryalus had 24 boats in tow from booms on each quarter. We proceeded to Gallipoli at 9pm at about 5 knots, arriving off there at about 3.30am on the morning of the 25th. Everyone was then called out and went to breakfast.

25th April

Anglo-French forces land on shores of Dardanelle straits.

Canon Andrews

We scrambled into our rowing boats around 3am Those of us who were to take the oars had been practising whilst waiting at Lemnos. Dawn was just breaking as we were about to land, fortunately at the wrong place, a steep rocky section of the coast where the Turks had no machine guns as they thought it quite impossible to land there. Just as we were disembarking somebody in the crowded boat shouted 'Can't land here water too deep', then a small shell landed in the bows and knocked out one or two and we were soon all in the water and swimming ashore.

Excerpt from Canon's Folly, *page* 56.

H M Wilson

The Lancashire's embarked at about 4am and shoved off at about 4.30. I was in charge of a picket boat and Alfred Williams in a steam pinnace. As we steamed slowly for the shore we gradually wheeled round to get opposite W Beach. Euryalus followed behind us but kept her distance, as there was a fear of shelling.

All the while the cliffs were being shelled but it turned out they weren't shelling quite the right place. It was just getting daylight and with the dawn mist it was quite hard to see what W beach was like or even where it was. We could not predict what sort of reception we were going to get. We stopped around 30 yards from the beach as we were nearly on the rocks.

The tows all pulled in front without fouling each other. There were two lines of barbed wire for the whole length of the beach. The Turks opened fire just as we stopped with maxims and rifles. You could see them standing up in their trenches which showed they could not have been properly shelled. They poured a terrific fire down on us and I can't understand how so many did in fact survive.

The soldiers had to jump out into about 3 feet of water and it was so terrible to see them being shot as soon as they were in the water. The wounded ones tried to hang on to the boats but most drowned, as there was nothing to do to help them. Those that got to the beach were of course held up by the barbed wire and this ensured even more casualties.

The Turks just mowed them down as they moved through the gaps in the wire they had just cut. They then had to take the cliffs each side, which were full of snipers and they had to rush about five sets of trenches, which followed straight after up the valley. The way they took the cliffs was splendid but they lost huge numbers doing it. The Turks could not face the bayonet and as soon as the Lancashire's got to the top 300 of them surrendered.

We made three mistakes: a) not shelling enough. b) not mounting guns in the picket boats as we had such a good view of them we could have provided good covering fire for the soldiers and c) the men should not have landed wearing all their equipment as it got in their way terribly.

However the Turks made mistakes too. They must have known we would land there, as it was one of 4 possible places. Our soldiers could have held the beach. They had not laid mines and they could have put extra barbed wire in the water. it is I think only our soldiers could have landed there. The landing at V beach was absolute slaughter. We lost 400 men in two hours and on V beach there were only 50 men left of the Munsters. Two midshipmen were killed and one wounded.

By the evening things had eased a little and we were able to get some of the wounded out but so many had drowned from very small wounds. The Australians were not taking prisoners and we were only taking a few. The French shot everyone. The picket boats were hit many times but the shield we had put up proved very effective. I feel it was miraculous we got any of them ashore at all. I went to the River Clyde in the evening to take off some of the wounded. The Turks opened fire as we were doing this and some of the wounded on stretchers where killed. I managed to get some sleep between 2.30 and 6.30, as I felt a bit done. During this time the French landed. They got about 400 prisoners whom they shot, as they were bored with looking after them.

Alfred Williams

I remember during the middle watch getting out of my hammock, stowing it, and going forward to my steam pinnace very carefully stepping over the Lancashire Fusiliers who were sleeping on the upper deck. I thought to myself, 'How many of these chaps will be dead or wounded within 2 hours?'

Before long our eight naval steam boats each got four life boats in tow with 25 fusiliers and 2 or 3 seamen in each lifeboat, making about 800 in all in the first landing.

The beach on which the Lancashires landed was called W beach on the landing plan, and this was changed afterwards to the 'Lancashire Landing'. There were seven picket boats, and one steam pinnace, which was mine on the right. She was the best steam pinnace in the fleet luckily, but we slowed the others up a bit even though we went flat out.

I was the midshipman in the steamboat, which took in the right hand tow, and as we got close in I looked down and found to my consternation there were rocks underneath me. No sand at all. It continued like that for a few moments and when I slipped my tow, I waved them on to the left where the rocks ended and sand began, and got out of it myself as quickly as I could.

The picket boats could go astern and keep fairly straight, but my steam pinnace had a tendency for the stern to kick off to port when I went astern, which made things extra difficult in order to keep out of the way of incoming cutters which I had been towing and slipped. The idea of running aground hard on rocks did not appeal to me at that moment and I only avoided that fate narrowly.

Several bullets struck the boat and one or two hit the shield behind which the coxswain and I were standing. I think the bulk of the rifle fire was concentrated on the life boats rather than on the steam boats and as far as I remember there were certainly some casualties before the boats grounded and of course a lot more on the beach and as they attacked up the hill. We then collected up the almost empty lifeboats and towed them out to the minelayers for some more soldiers. Being minelayers they were shallow and could come in closer than other ships. I was soon landing a second lot of soldiers.

During that day a naval Captain called, I think, Collard had trouble with the temporary pier that he was building on W beach and he called me in to help him. As a Midshipman I could not disobey the order of a naval Captain and went to help. I worked flat out under his orders 'tending' any sort of craft that came alongside.

In the meantime my coxswain 'stood off' to wait for me in the steam pinnace, in which position he came under heavier fire from Turkish rifle bullets which came over the British trenches than we did on the pier, and so he went back to Euryalus.

For 24 hours onboard Euryalus everyone thought I was killed or missing. One of the other midshipman called Tatham, who came from South Africa, was in the naval landing party at the Lancashire Landing, and he did very good work during the first night taking up boxes of ammunition to the trenches.

I did not find very much to do during the night, but I do remember sitting down on a big cheese. I soon got up from it, but I stank of cheese until I changed my trousers, and was not very popular during that period.

In talking of Anzac Day it is useful to remember the relative casualties suffered on the various beaches, and these of course can only be approximate. But the idea of those of us who took part in any of the landings at the time was that the Dublin and Munster Fusiliers, landing from the River Clyde on V beach suffered the heaviest casualties.

The Lancashire Fusiliers suffered the next heaviest casualties and the Anzacs suffered the third heaviest. I mean actually in the first 24 hours of fighting.

The Dublin's and Munsters poured out from the bows of the River Clyde down gangways over lighters and onto V Beach. They suffered very heavy casualties indeed before they got clear of the beach. There was a small bank on top of the beach, and I think they were kept under that until darkness came. Or at any rate some of them were.

I know a little more about the Lancashire Fusiliers as I was there. This body of men suffered a number of casualties and this was thought because they were towed in boats facing aft so they went into action with their backs to the enemy which was unusual. Very soon after this the Flag Lieutenant went ashore to organise signal communications between navy and army and I went back to Euryalus.

When I got back onboard I realised for the first time how fond of us midshipmen the officers were. Lieutenant Godfrey who had looked very sad when saying goodbye to us as we went to our boats and started to take our tows told me afterwards that he thought he was sending us all to certain death. He was very distressed about it.

For this affair all the midshipmen got DSCs but I think we all felt that every one of the Lancashire Fusiliers deserved an award far more than we did. Once they had got to the top of the cliffs, the boats coming in and out and landing reinforcements from the minesweepers didn't have to suffer very much more from the rifle fire.

As April 25th drew to a close I felt I had no cause for self-congratulation. Euryalus stayed on at Gallipoli until one day a periscope was spotted and we scuttled for safety once again. In our case we went through the Suez Canal after which we felt completely safe.

It must have been so depressing for the soldiers on Gallipoli to see the Navy depart. Our guns with flat trajectories were not really suitable for bombarding the Turkish trenches and I don't really know how effective we were. At any rate the noise and smoke created had been a comfort to the army but it would have been stupid for us to stay on once the U boats started turning up.

Alfred Williams
Another diary entry.

At 4.15am the Battalion of the Lancashire Fusiliers, consisting of about 840 officers and men got into boats, and at 5.00am they proceeded towards 'W' Beach followed closely by Euryalus. On the left a similar force was starting from Implacable, but eventually landed on 'V' Beach.

On our right the River Clyde with 2,000 men on board was steaming for 'V' Beach in company with another force in boats from H.M.S. Cornwallis. As the boats started, the covering ships commenced bombarding. No fire from the shore was opened on the boats at 'W' Beach until they were 100 yards off or perhaps closer. The boats were slipped when they were 150 to 200 yards from the shore. It was found later that they might have been slipped closer in but under those conditions of uncertainty it would have been unsafe to slip them closer in-shore. (What this meant, I think, was that if the steam boats hit the rocks, they would have been out of action and unable to go back and tow in the reinforcements from the mine-sweepers.)

The boats were well together and the landing was safely accomplished. The men, when once ashore, advanced despite heavy rifle fire and machine gun fire and barbed wire entanglements. They reached the top of the cliffs and took the trenches there with a courage and gallantry that I should think had seldom if ever been surpassed in military history. (This sounds very pompous for a boy of under 18, and it was probably partly cribbed from a signal).

When established at the top of the cliff the Lancashire Fusiliers held on there till reinforced. In the meantime as soon as the boats were emptied they shoved off and were either pulled or were towed out to the fleet-sweepers that were as close inshore as possible. They discharged their wounded and took the supporting troops on board and were towed in again to shore. This continued till 7.30am when the fleet-sweepers were emptied and they went out to the transports which were lying 2 or 3 miles off, for more troops. The boats were laid off out of range of snipers.

After the first 800 were ashore the firing diminished to a large extent though there must have been a number of snipers hiding in holes in the cliffs. They devoted some of their attention to the sweepers and fifteen or twenty casualties must have been caused by them in the sweepers and in the boats waiting along side them.

After about half an hour the sweepers returned, and were unloaded as before. In the afternoon provision and ammunition lighters came in and made fast to buoys and ropes which had been laid out to the beach by trawlers, and the beach party which had been landed in the second landing from the sweepers, hauled them ashore and unloaded them. Shortly after, guns, horses, and mules were landed. In the meantime a landing had been successfully accomplished at 'X' Beach with small loss. This was probably due to a most thorough and effective bombardment of the beach and cliffs before the boats went in.

Canon Andrews

By the end of the first day the Anzacs had a footing on the peninsula and some of the Australian units had advanced several miles inland. Stretcher-bearers had been busy all day and I was settling down under the cliff on the beach in the evening when I was sent for. It was to ask me if I would go and bury the dead. A party of men was given to me to dig the graves. Accompanied by gunfire in the distance both on the land and at sea, we buried them by night in one great big grave; there was no time to separate the Protestants from the Catholics.

Notes taken from Canon's Folly, *page 57.*

27th April

In Ypres the Allies' attack is halted by gas.

30th April

Germany warns US against sailing the Lusitania.

1st May

Turks attack allied line at Gallipoli.

4th May

H M Wilson

Dear Mother,

We continue to land supplies and horses. A lot more troops are expected. I am trying to get hold of a Turkish rifle or bayonet. I am so glad to have been out here as Williams and I landed the very first lot.

We have not had any mails for about 10 days. The Turks are such a dirty lot. Their trenches were a disgrace. So untidy and that was with us having missed shelling them! We have around 1000 prisoners.

Your loving son,

Hubert

7th May

Lusitania torpedoed off south west coast of Ireland. Nearly 2000 drowned.

10th May

Anti German demonstrations in London in aftermath of Lusitania sinking.

19th May

Age limit for recruits set at 40.

23rd May

Italy declares war against Austria.

25th May

HMS Triumph torpedoed at Gallipoli.

Canon Andrews

The endless days and weeks went by, the weather becoming hotter as we hung onto the territory we had gained, making little progress in spite of many local attacks with heavy casualties. Our hope was with the ships of the Navy in the background sailing majestically backwards and forwards.

Early one morning we looked out to sea and found the Queen Elizabeth with her 'ladies in waiting' had disappeared. The German submarines were near. Triumph remained close until one morning she lurched forward as if stabbed in the back and smoke burst upward from her side. She had been hit. We stood and watched her crew get off her as she rolled over and within eleven minutes she was gone. Ships came and went and the fight went on. German submarines caused havoc not only to the battleships that protected us but also the convoys getting food to us. Rations became scarce and we all began to lose weight.

Notes taken from Canon's Folly, *page 58.*

31st May

Zeppelin raid on London.

2nd June

Attacks on Gallipoli continue.

W H Carver

In June the Battalion marched from Hornsea to Ripon camp for large-scale divisional training. Training was mainly for open warfare because static trench warfare was not expected to last much longer on the Western Front.

Notes taken from The Trench, *page 32.*

20th June

C Carver
Heytesbury

My darling mum,

I do hope you haven't minded me not writing before but I simply didn't have the time. I had a good journey down and somehow found my way to Divisional Headquarters where I saw General Stone commanding the Artillery. I am posted to the 84th Brigade. We have just returned from manoeuvres. It's all good fun and the fellows are all nicer than the ones at Weedon. We are just putting on the finishing touches before pushing off for France or the Dardanelles. The King inspected us last Thursday, which is usually a pretty sure sign you will soon be off.

Tonnes of love from,

Crick

Canon Andrews

Ration shortages also meant a shortage of water from Malta. I carried on taking services and burying the dead. My days at Gallipoli then came to a sudden end. I became very ill and was taken by hospital ship to Mudros on the island of Lemnos, which was gradually transforming into a large rest camp and hospital. While there I continued to get worse and was put on another hospital ship to Malta.

Notes taken from Canon's Folly, *page 59 – 61.*

Robert Williams

Robert Williams arrives in France with the Grenadier Guards.

Alfred Williams

On the Euryalus I took on duty as a sort of junior Flag Lieutenant. In fact, the Chief Yeoman did all the work and I was really just a messenger taking signals from the bridge to anyone onboard who was interested in them. I well remember taking a signal down to the Rear Admiral 'Rosy' Wemyss who happened to be in a steam bath and the steam apparatus burst as I arrived with my signal. Luckily he was not hurt but I had rather a complete view of him and it was difficult not to laugh. He was a terribly nice man who was loved by all who served him. Once at Port Said we went from war conditions to peace conditions. All the brass had been painted with grey paint. This was now all taken off and bluebell polish was once again in full use. We went down to the Red Sea, over to Bombay, and then onto Trincomalee and over to Penang. It was here I came close to a diseased beggar who had a hole for a nose. This sight probably did me more good than a lot of sermons did me. We then came back to Colombo and having completed our time as midshipmen, eight of us were to go back home by P & O liner, which would have been great fun. But Euryalus was ordered back to Suez so we went back in her to Aden and then from there to Alexandria and stayed there for 8 months.

Tudor St John

One day Tudor was wheeled in on a chair and lined up with half a dozen others to be presented to the King and Queen. Wounded officers in those day wore civilian cloths – the inevitable Marlborough jacket and Bowler – and as the couple came down the line shaking hands, Tudor with difficulty got him self standing with the aid of two sticks, putting his bowler on the seat behind so as to have a hand free. Seeing how frail he was the King told him to sit down, and in his relief Tudor forgot about the hat and started to subside gratefully into his wheelchair. Queen Mary close behind the monarch and spotting the impending disaster leapt forward and with rapier sharp parasol, made as if to knock the bowler hat out of harms way, but instead succeeded in impaling it like a brochette and waving aloft much to everyone's delight – King George's in particular. Notes taken from A Tale of Two Rivers.

26th July

C Carver

My darling Mum,

Here we are off at last. We reach Southampton about 12.30 and will embark around 3.00pm. The crossing takes 24 hours. We then have 24 hours at Le Havre and then on by train to a concentration area somewhere behind the firing line, which we will not get into for at least a fortnight. It has poured for days and the camp was a sea of mud when we left it. Please thank dad very much for the gloves,

Tonnes of love,

Christian

28th July

C Carver

My darling Mum,

Thanks awfully for your letter. We have had a splendid time so far including the crossing. We are well behind the line but are going into reserve and thence quickly into it. The Germans have been in this village but only for a few hours before the turn of the tide. When we were disembarking the horses I took them to the square in front of the prison ship (crammed with German prisoners of war). I have never seen a collection of men looking so bored before. The number of flies and rats is truly singular (or rather very plural). I should like it if you could manage a weekly hamper of cake, sweets, cigarettes, matches, magazines, and papers. If you could fix this up I can send a cheque along every now and then and you can take the expenses out of it. Any remainder would be welcome back but in Francs please. All such additions to the mess are all thankfully received and you might spread this among friends. I have found that in England I never appreciated drinkable water. We have to drink out of a water cart and it has a taste of chlorine in it. We are strictly forbidden to say where we are or whether we have been in action. But we are moving along tomorrow further up. We had an inter-section cricket match this afternoon. Thanks awfully for your letters.

Tonnes of love from,

Christian

31st July

Ten-day movement of German troops from Eastern to Western Front completed.

3rd August

C Carver

My dear old Hump,

On Monday we moved on up 12 miles and were told we were to bivouac in preparation for action the following night. However the crowd we are relieving have not gone yet so we will probably not begin fighting for a week. You see we simply take over the position of another Battery who have just scattered their guns about any old how and covered them up with tarpaulins to make them look like disused mowers I suppose. The men live in caves dug in the roadside. We have got a nice observation station in the wood but cannot see the whole of the German trench from it and we have to have three in our trench, which is 50 yards away from the German trench. We are at present in a cornfield and very comfortable. It's now too dark to write.

Tonnes of love to all,

from Crick

5th August

C Carver
Bellevue

My beloved Mum,

They never seem to let us stay in the same place and we have moved on again. My section will go into action in 2 or 3 days. We are missing our English news a lot, as we have had no communications for a day or two. Thanks awfully for your letters. I am anxious to get going.

Shots are rare and matters are at a stalemate here but 'shell first, shell hard, and keep on shelling' is going to be our motto judging from the noise and flashes last night.

Tonnes of love from,

Christian

PS We saw our first glimpse of war yesterday, an aeroplane being shelled vigorously (I don't know which side it was but it got away).

8th August

HMS Ramsay and India attacked. Naval General Service medal instituted.

C Carver
Bellevue

My darling Mum,

I have been eagerly awaiting the next mail which has been chasing us around. I am here in charge of the section that has not gone into action.

The men have got a very comfortable camp on the riverbank where I write this, and much washing and swimming is done. My section does not go into action till the 13th but I have been promised that I will be relieved and can go up earlier.

If only there was not a war on and I could speak French, life would be ideal. I am so full of life and vigour that the wily Bosche who pushes me out will have to get up pretty early in the morning. I daresay plenty of them do though. Make sure you all write to me to your hearts content as there maybe nothing to do for days.

Tonnes of love,

Christian

10th August

C Carver
Bellevue
In the firing line at last

My beloved Mum,

I have just got your two letters for which many thanks, as one does not appreciate letters until one gets out here. Thanks also for the literature and the food which went down well at the billets. I write this up with the guns as we have just been doing some firing and three hours later are just doing some more.

We came into action here last night under somewhat unpropitious circumstances but have had a splendid day today and have bagged something I hope. Give ear unto the manner in which the left section came into action.

On Monday we got orders to move at 7.45pm and got into action at once on arrival after an 8-mile march. It didn't appear we had been expected which was rather cheering. To add to this an electrical storm was in progress. The dugouts are comfortable and each has a bomb proof shelter. Please thank the family for the parcels I have received.

TONS of love from,

Christian

11th August

British attack of Gallipoli ends.

H M Wilson

Dear Mother,

We are off once more to Gallipoli and are hoping for another good show having been doing very little for three months. The weather is hot and we bathe all the time. We have been wearing whites, which is nice. However the stores of fresh food are very low to non-existent.

My teeth are full of holes. I can't believe this time last year I was so keen to see some action and now I have. I saw in The Times today about my DSC. It was the first I had heard about it when I got your wire. I hope you saw that Williams got one too. He was in our other steamboat.

Your loving son,

Hubert

15th August

C Carver
Bellevue

My very beloved Mum,

Thanks awfully for your letters. I usually get 2 from you and one from dad by each post. We have had just a week in action and on the whole have had jolly good sport. We do 24 hour shifts in the trenches and then with the guns. We have taken over from the French who had dug themselves ripping trenches so we are very comfortable here. The trenches are about 50 yards apart and things are very quiet, not dull mind you. Night is the busy time for the infantry. We have a good binocular periscope and can see a number of the Hun's buttons and how hard he is working etc. When I was up yesterday I 'strafed' one working party of 12 men with a nice little shrapnel; my aunt they went to ground like rabbits. We have not had any shells very near the battery yet. I cannot claim any narrow escapes in the trenches except for the snipers when one puts ones head above the parapet for too long. I will write when I have time.

Tonnes of love,

Crick

Canon Andrews

By the middle of August I was fully recovered and then sent to Alexandria again. I was told I would be appointed Army Chaplain as soon as I was well enough to return to England. In Alexandria I stayed in the Windsor Hotel till my orders came through confirming this appointment. From that moment on there was never a dull moment.

Notes taken from Canon's Folly, *page 62.*

17th August

Robert Williams

Dear Didden,

I have just seen today's Times and I cannot tell you how glad I am to see you both getting the DSC and also mentioned. You must be very pleased and rightly so; it is the best news I have had since the war began. At the same time it will be the best possible news for both Father and Mother. Time is short.

Your affectionate brother,

RW

18th August

Russian naval success in Baltic. German fleet retires.

20th August

Italy declares war on Turkey. German fleet penetrates the Gulf.

C Carver
In the trenches at Bellevue

My darling mum,

Thanks once more for all the letters. It makes such a difference to get all the loving letters that I do get. We have had a very quiet time in the trenches today but they shelled us pretty heavily yesterday.

Tonnes and stacks of love to all,

Crick

Alfred Williams

Dear Didden,

My warmest congratulations on the honour you have obtained and my only wish is that you may be preserved through the awful war long enough to enjoy it. I have heard from your parents and you must know how delighted they are about it.

You must have seen some terrible scenes during that landing from all we can gather from the papers. Things are very sad at home and will be until the war is over as the anxiety of so many must be very great.

Your affectionate Uncle.

23rd August

Week of air raids begins.

C Carver
In the trenches at Bellevue

My dear Dad,

I write this while waiting to pepper a large wood in which Germans have been doing a lot of work lately; they won't be so enthusiastic in future. Watching the enemy's country through a periscope always reminds me of Alice looking into the looking glass and wondering what went on in the parts she couldn't see. The country seems so peaceful and quiet with apparently not a soul in sight and yet just beyond the parapet any amount of activity is invariably going on.

Tonnes of love,

Christian

24th August

C Carver
In the trenches
Bellevue

My most beloved Mum,

Thanks awfully for your last letter. Could you send me some stout khaki thread, boot polish, button polish and also a clothes brush? The trenches are awful for tearing ones clothes as they are narrow and there is wire projecting everywhere. We had a great shoot last night at some working parties in the wood. It was good news about the Russian victory in the Baltic. I hope it will buck them up a bit.

Tonnes of love from,

Crick

3rd September

Canon Andrews

I hadn't been long at The Windsor Hotel when I met a man called Oswin Creighton. He insisted that I should not be hanging around for orders from bishops in England. He rather felt they had no idea there was a war on and encouraged me to help him with the care of all the sick men from Gallipoli that were dying of boredom on Mudros.

He realised it wouldn't be long until there were ten thousand men there and with no canteens and entertainment he felt the place needed brightening up. He wrote to London requesting £1000 for his venture. It was finalised I should go with him back to Lemnos and not wait to go back to England.

From that moment on we were hardly separated, rushing about buying pianos and gramophones. Never have I seen such energy from someone. His aim was to create places on Lemnos where the wounded could go and forget the war.

Notes taken from Canon's Folly, *page 63.*

C Carver
In our Observing post
Bellevue

My dear Dad,

I am afraid it is some time since I wrote. We have had a lot of cold wet weather these last few days and there is mud mud mud everywhere. There is no doubt we much prefer shell to rain, as you can at least get away from shells. On our left is what was once a prosperous town but it is in ruins now and its church's spire is hanging off at a most peculiar angle.

The valley is full of wriggling white lines running back for one main one, these being communication trenches. About 50 yards on are the enemy's trenches running twist for twist with ours. By the way I would be awfully grateful if you could get hold of some waders for me, as they are absolutely the thing for trenches. If they are to be got I will send a cheque. Well, goodbye for the present and tonnes of love to all,

Christian

5th September

13th day of incessant bombardment comes to an end on Western Front. Australians repulse Turkish attacks in the Dardanelles.

6th September

C Carver

Dear Mum,

Thanks awfully for your letters. We have just survived two rounds of 'hate' from Fat Fritz. The 'hate' takes the form of a distant bang, then whooooooooooo BANG! Large fountains of earth 25 yards in front of the battery spew up while bits of shell fuse, stone etc whiz over head accompanied by shrieks of laughter and groans of derision from the great untouched.

Meanwhile the Huns write home to say they have annihilated another Battery and England will be sure to give up soon. I had an interesting day yesterday as I managed to watch the Germans relieve their trenches. I could see them sweating up hill in marching order and getting on bicycles and riding off. We got a note from the sappers yesterday to say they were popping off a mine at 7.30pm.

Good, we said, just time to see it before dinner. So off we went at a convenient place on the right flank. Just imagine a wet cold evening, just not quite dark and ourselves waiting to see a few Huns propelled skywards; do you envy us our harmless little pleasures?

Prompt at 7.30 two dirty looking flames appeared on the horizon followed by a horrible tearing cracking noise, then about a dozen magnesium lights. The place was then covered in a dense smoke and finally a great burst of rifle fire came from both sides. Both sides try for the crater but of course the side who blew it have a distinct advantage. At this juncture the stray bullets became so unpleasantly numerous that we decamped to our dinner not without haste.

Tonnes of love,

Crick

7th September

C Carver
In the OP

My dear Mum,

After a lot of beastly wet we are having it fine again. Hot in the daytime but jolly cold at night. Things still jog along quietly enough and neither of us seems to do much harm, which is an obvious development. If you hurt Fritz he simply hurts you back and this is unnecessary wastage. I have decided we must have a Battery gramophone. I must have got pretty good credit. I had £54 at Cox's and have only drawn 125 Francs since then. I shall want around £60 after the war to get my dress uniform. Well au revoir.

TOL,

Crick

9th September

H M Wilson

My dear Mother,

Many thanks for all your letters. If you would like you can write DSC after my name. There are all sorts of tales about the Italians coming out here but no one knows for certain. The Balkan States are the people who really matter. They will make all the difference. I haven't discovered what sort of coloured ribbon the medal will be on. I hope you won't be angry but I have applied to do submarines. They are just as safe as what I am doing at the moment. And I always wanted to before war broke out. I would get £40 a year if I managed it, which isn't bad for 18. We have just got some fresh food, which couldn't have come sooner as we were all getting dysentery.

Your loving son,

Hubert

11th September

Zeppelin raid at night on the east coast.

C Carver

My dear Mum and Dad,

Thanks most awfully for the letters and the waders, they are just the thing, though I may need stronger ones for the winter. The section of trench we are in and the Huns trench run through a village though its former inhabitants are unlikely to recognise it. I got into the middle of a lump of hate this morning but escaped with some rubbish down my neck. I knew I should get it in the neck sooner or later. I write this at 5.35pm and at 5.45 there is going to be a 'Strafe'. An intrepid lad called Ellis has smuggled up one of his guns to within 200 yards of a beastly little hot bed of a sniper's gallery. They are going to loose off 30 rounds and then run for their lives if indeed they have any to run for. Rather a sporting effort. There he goes now. It is not likely to be one-sided and I am sure we will chip in with the odd round. It is a beastly place. Both trenches run though a wood and at one point they both share the same parapet. That is an absolute fact. It is a jumpy place to be and the odd mine that goes up adds to the excitement. We have heard a lot of rumours lately of the Dardanelles being forced but are probably as unreliable as most rumours are.

Tonnes of love to you my dearest Mum and Dad,

Crick

16th September

Robert Williams

Dear Didden,

Many thanks for the letters. I am very pleased it was a letter of mine, which told you of your DSC for that will naturally be one of the great steps in your life. I doubt if you realise how pleased father and mother and all of us were at your getting it. As to sending you chocolates I only wish I was able to send you more but that cannot be. No. 8 has not yet been in a trench but we have been in billets for the last 7 weeks. As you will see by my address I am now away from the 3rd G.Guards and am part of a machine gun company. Naturally as it has only been formed some three days I cannot say how it will work but I hope to get a nice time in every way, and I think we shall be better looked after and we should make more effect than we did before. Naturally I can give no local news and for that matter we know very little, but personally I expect to have my fill of fighting long before this reaches you. With all best wishes,

Your affectionate brother,

R Williams

H M Wilson
HMS Skate

My dear Father,

I have just been here a week and I think I shall like it very much. It is ever so much better than my last ship though the job is much the same. The Captain is a very good sort, which is a good thing in such a small ship. I expect you saw Williams was mentioned in dispatches. I had lunch with his brother the other day in town – the one who stood for Northwich. I am afraid one can't say much about what we are doing.

Your affectionate son,

Hubert

25th September

Great Allied Offensive begins (Loos and Champagne).

John Williams

Dear Didden,

I was very glad to get your letter. I heard from mother that you hadn't been very well but I hope you are better now. Matters out your way seem very mixed. I am glad you like Weymss as he was the captain of Osborne when I was first there and was very popular.

You ought to try and make a point of keeping in touch with him now that you have got to know him as it is sure to get you a long way with any luck, and a man like that is more help in the way of getting on than you probably realise now. I hope you have received the chocolate I sent you. When do you expect to get promoted? Many thanks for your letter.

Your loving brother,

John F Williams

C Carver
In the trenches Saturday

My very beloved mum,

I feel a brute mark I for not writing before. My only excuse has been lack of time and unsuitable environment. I have not changed boots or clothes since Tuesday and it has rained all the time. I have just received a load of earth down my neck. At present we are bombarding merrily and considerable changes are in prospect – lets hope it all comes off. We are building new gun pits quite close behind here and I usually trot around ours twice a day to see the progress. We are building a dummy hedge to screen us from Fritz and shall probably dash in and bang off a thousand rounds and exit. It will be a question of minutes before he gets onto us. Thanks awfully for your letters.

TONS of love from,

Christian

26th September

British defence holds against attacks around Loos.

27th September

Successful attack by Guards at Loos.

30th September

French gain more ground at Champagne. Fighting around Loos continues.

C Carver

My very beloved Mum,

I shall be able to write more now that I am out of the trenches for a bit. It is impossible to write a decent letter in them. On the evening we arrived here we had a heavy bombardment and then were given the message 'enemy advancing fi left' I hastily filled my revolver but after half an hour nothing had happened but it made me realise to always have my revolver ready. The Germans have been very comic lately. After we had been strafing them a good bit they put up a sign with 'chuck it' written on it. They love putting up targets and signalling a miss for every shot fired. Yesterday they put up a row of eight stones along their parapet and a Sergeant Major who is a crack shot started knocking them off from left to right. After he had done 4 they picked the rest up and threw them at us! Under all this however runs a tragic vein. While I was down here there were 12 causalities among the men. I had got in from digging at 11 o'clock one night and was told one of the officers had been badly hit out on patrol and that they were trying to get him in. He had gone out with a bomber to try and settle a troublesome sniper when almost on the German wire they ran into a patrol. The officer got a bullet through his shoulder and both lungs. The bomber was so jolted he ran back for help and four times they went out again under heavy machine gun fire to bring the officer back. A little further along the line was his elder brother who was told and he came down and went out a fifth time to try and get him back. As a matter of chance he fell into the very shell hole his brother was lying in and they got him back and put him on my bed but he must have been dead for over three hours poor chap. Could you send me some warmer clothes as things are turning distinctly chilly. Please don't think I am not enjoying life. I am. Of course if you try and read between the lines of this brainless scrawl to find some indication that my life is being blighted you are bound to hit on something. I can tell you I extract the maximum enjoyment out of things that I can. We go into reserve tomorrow which I am not sorry for as it gives us a fortnight away from the trenches.

Tons of love to all,

Crick

Canon Andrews

Eventually a ship to Lemnos was scheduled so Oswin decided to sail with all his purchases. We spent a rushed three days getting together tents and marquees. We got him and his gear on board and I waved him goodbye. I knew I should miss his freshness and energy and unswerving faith. He returned some time later still overflowing with energy and enthusiasm. When he returned back to Lemnos he took me and we began in earnest to sort out the canteens.

Notes taken from Canon's Folly, *page* 66.

1st October

Robert Williams 3rd Battalion Grenadier Guards Diary.

Left trenches at Vergigneul after very tiring tour of duty. Col. Corry returned.

2nd October

Robert Williams 3rd Battalion Grenadier Guards Diary.

Rest day.

3rd October

Enemy captures part of Hohenzollern Redout at Loos. Russia gives ultimatum to Bulgaria.

Robert Williams 3rd Battalion Grenadier Guards Diary.

Moved forward again to so-called billets in the ruined village of Vermelles. Terrific noise from our own guns with occasional bursts of shelling from the enemy.

4th October

Allies give ultimatum to Bulgaria.

Robert Williams 3rd Battalion Grenadier Guards Diary.

In the evening took over front line trenches. Very wet and dark night. Took ten hours to get into our places. Very complicated plan of half finished trenches. Dug day and night but difficult to make the position even reasonably secure.

5th October

British attack north of Loos.

Robert Williams 3rd Battalion Grenadier Guards Dairy.

In front line Trenches.

6th October

Robert Williams 3rd Battalion Grenadier Guards Diary.

In front line Trenches.

7th October

Heavy indecisive fighting at Champayne and Argonne. British Labour leaders appeal for volunteers for army.

Robert Williams 3rd Battalion Grenadier Guards Diary.

In front line Trenches.

8th October

Important German attack near Loos repulsed. Huge enemy losses.

Robert Williams 3rd Battalion Grenadier Guards Diary.

In the afternoon were heavily attacked all along the line. The enemy bombers rushed our left flank and came bombing down our line. They surprised and surrounded our own bombers killing most of them. Sergeant Williams who was commanding a machine gun was killed and three successive machine gun sergeants were also killed. The two Companies were ordered to retire down the communication trenches to make way for the bombers of the Cold Stream Guards. They managed to stop the advance and clear the enemy out and the trenches were reoccupied after the attack was over. It was repulsed along the whole line with great loss of life to both sides.

Colonel Corry writes to Colonel Streatfield, Commander of the Grenadier Guards:

Williams killed in the 'Big Willie' action at Loos. What a splendid fellow and a great loss.

Captain Claud Bartholomew wrote:

Your son did extremely well as I expected he would. After all the men on one of his guns had been killed or wounded he fired it himself until hit and was killed instantaneously. Mr Williams had only been in my company six or seven weeks but he impressed us all with his keenness and enthusiasm. I shall feel his loss as a Company Officer very greatly.

10th October

Scattered fighting along most of front line.

C Carver

My very darling mum,

I went for a ride with Carroll today behind the lines and the horses were very fresh and nearly pulled our arms out. On our right was a Frenchman with three white horses shouting something unintelligibly at them. Behinds us was the road along which is a continuous trickle of British soldiers that gets greater during the night. Ladies and children were accompanied by dogs on our left, as they appeared to be digging at a cabbage patch. They scarper when Bosche starts shelling. After a committee meeting I have been asked to provide in the fullness of time 134 mufflers. I wonder if you know of anyone who is keen on making mufflers. I assure you that I do enjoy life here. I wake up every morning feeling happy without a care in the world. What is there to care about anyway? A few shells but one gets used to them. The only thing I don't like is the trenches and the fear of being gassed with nowhere to run. Oh I could and do enjoy anything after the trenches. It brings one up with a jerk to think that it's one's profession to kill one's fellow man across the way. What wicked madness it all seems. Well goodnight and all my love, from,

Christian

17th October

C Carver

My darling Mum,

Thanks awfully for your letter. We had rather a scare lately about these white horses, which do the ploughing. Said to be a means of signalling and they certainly shelled 2 Batteries, which the white horses, were in line with. All investigated and found authentic however. They do have a good spy system the Huns. Well goodbye till Friday, as I don't think I will be mentally able to write from the trenches.

Tons of love,

Crick

19th October

Italy declares war against Bulgaria.

20th October

John Williams

Dear Didden,

You will have heard by now of Bob's death in France. Well I suppose it was as fine an end as he or any of us could have wished for and as father says we should think how lucky we have been in having had such a brother and having known such a man. My ship is refitting at Belfast and very luckily I came on first leave and got down here two days after father but I had not heard from him, as our mails were adrift. Things seem very interesting and complicated out your way and one wonders what Greece will do. The threat of the navy should make her mind her manners.

Your affectionate brother,

John F Williams

Robert Williams
3rd Battalion Grenadier Guards
BEF, France

My dear Mr Williams,

I will try and tell you all I know of your son's end.

On the afternoon of the 8th the Germans bombarded the trenches we were holding and your son was near the gun on our dangerous flank. The Germans attacked with bombs at 4.30 and succeeded in entering the trench that your son was in. His gun was doing splendid work though the machine gunners were suffering heavily. Hawke was killed and then Kendrick came back from No. 2 Company to take his place and no sooner had he got up to serve the gun than he was killed. The Germans were getting very near the gun, and your son held on till the last, and then decided to retire. His team had been practically wiped out, so he carried the gun himself, and a private soldier took away the tripod. Mr Bowes-Lyon saw him then go down a communication trench carrying the gun. He got the gun away, and on reaching another trench, he turned round and patted the private soldier on the back and said, 'Well done, we have got it away.' No sooner had he said this than he was hit in the head with a bullet, and died at once. All I have said is as much as I can find out about his last few moments. I was sent up to this communication trench that night and I found his body just over the parapet where it had been put, while the attack was still on. One man in getting it back the next day was sniped through the head, but we eventually got him back and that night (Saturday) his body was moved to Vermelles. He was buried on Sunday at 2.30 in the Vermelles Cemetery and most of the officers were present. It was a short service and we laid him to rest in blankets, and the grave has been duly marked. Words cannot express what I feel for you in your great loss.

Your son was very much beloved and his men adored him. His energy was quite inexhaustible in educating his team and he lavished every kindness on them. He was a very fine machine gunner and we all lament his loss. If I hear any further particulars I will forward them at once. Please accept my deepest sympathy over the loss, and may you find some consolation in that your son died fighting, doing his duty, bravely and courageously to the end.

From one of his fellow officers,

H. Douglas Vernon.

Vernon was later killed in action on the 15th September 1916 aged 23 during the third great British advance on the Somme.

22nd October

C Carver

My very very darling Mum,

Thanks yet again for the letters. I had a fairly quiet time in the trenches except that the Huns blew up a colossal mine in front of us killing 10 people and wounding many more by gas poisoning. It is thought it may have gone off by mistake. It is a full moon tonight which makes it bad for the patrols.

I hear you're having the same fog we are having. As a matter of fact fog in the trenches is rather fun as you can walk about the ground between our own fire and the communication trenches and I even ventured forth in front of our own barbed wire. Funny to think I was only 30 seconds away from the German trenches.

Lots of love,

Christian

23rd October

King George appeals for more men. 'The end is not yet in sight.'

C Carver

My dear Bro,

Many thanks for your letters. Oh by the way you don't happen to have 134 mufflers on you? No? Well ask your friends will you because I am collecting them. Oh no not entirely for myself don't you know. I have started a great anti-rat campaign. First of all I put oatmeal down to allay suspicion. The next night the oatmeal is put down well laced with raticide. This is harmless to dogs and cats but in rats it breeds a deadly virus. Let us say one eats the oatmeal he then has 8 to 14 days before he leaves his home under my bed and dies in agony in the open. He is then devoured by a party of his particular friends say 5 pals and twenty mice who are then in turn all infected. Next 75% of the mice will be eaten by rats which are thus infected so that by the integral of calculus, 3011.3 rats will be suffering in three months time, which is very pleasing, in fact 'today's beautiful thought'. There is nothing of interest doing here as you have doubtless already gathered.

TOL from,

CCC

28th October

C Carver

My darling Mum,

Not much to report other than the weather has come in again. The area was still quite pretty when the Captain and I walked over today and did some registering. There is a chateau in the woods but gives the appearance it is no longer resided in due to lack of roof and front. Nothing can spoil the autumn tints in the woods though. Well goodnight now my darling mum and I can tell you that all the love that reaches me is very deeply appreciated.

Very much love from,

Christian

W H Carver

In early November the division was sent to Salisbury Plain for final training before posting overseas. Temporary command was handed over once more to Carver as Colonel Richardson felt he was too old to be allowed to go to France. They were allowed to rid themselves of their outdated rifles and began digging, occupying and relieving trenches on the Plain. They would march up past Stonehenge on the way to the 'Front'. They were about to leave England for active service overseas, not to France, as all had expected, but to Port Said and

Egypt. They would not reach the front line on the Somme till March 1916 when as part of a division they were to take part in the major new offensive planned for the first of July 1916.

Notes taken from The Trench, *page 33.*

4th November

Fierce fighting in Champagne

C Carver

My very darling Mum,

Thanks awfully for your letters. I am afraid poor old Serbia's number is up at least for the present though she will probably take more squashing than Belgium did. I believe the Germans have chucked in all ideas of pushing on this front, at any rate here. We can't chuck it in though and I do hope we get a chance for some open fighting.

Tons of love to all,

Crick

Stephen Williams

Stephen Williams was commissioned in 1915 aged 19 into the Royal Horse Artillery, the elite of the gunner regiment. He wrote his First World War accounts while in a prisoner of war camp in Tobruk in the Second World War.

Whilst training at 'The Shop' we boys dreaded that the war might end before we had an opportunity of serving, not then foreseeing the enormity of the experiences awaiting us. Consequently it was with enthusiasm that, on being commissioned, most of us joined batteries in the newly formed 'Kitchener's Army'. In my own case the 112th Brigade of the 25th Infantry Division, who were then at their final shooting practise on Salisbury Plain preliminary to sailing over seas.

That initial visit to Lanark Ranges was a welcome introduction to the area and the many happier days to be spent sometime later on. At that time the Plain was burdened with camps and alive with general military activity, whilst away in the seclusion of the dangers of the target area was a small herd of deserter horses and mules, who had decided to soldier no more and continued to evade arrest for the remainder of the war.

Newcomers naturally served in the rear party on the divisional shipment which entailed rejoining late by passing through the army base at Le Havre. What an eye opener that was, to see so many thousands of officers and men without anything to do, who were bursting with keenness to get up into the fighting line.

Amongst the imposing spectacle of a great hearted crowd was an insignificant sprinkling of real bad brutes that made good things for themselves out of an atmosphere of general irresponsibility. These parasites ran remunerative gambling cliques, the game of 'House' never ceased to play in every compound, and without doubt some of the non-commissioned officers officiating there were having a rake out of the spoils.

The base was a natural dumping ground for 'swingers' and 'shirkers' of many kinds, which made it an increasingly unsavoury place for a decent soldier. It was also the deposit for military criminals undergoing that peculiar and severe Field Punishment No 1, that of being tied and crucified by wrists and ankles to a wheel twice a day.

There was not much glamour in the carnage of the trenches. One of the saddest things for me, apart from many of my young friends being killed, was the slaughter of so many fine horses; all guns and transport were pulled by horses and all the best and most favourite of people's hunters were requisitioned.

The 25th Division took over the section of trench line from Armentieres north to Ploegstreet wood, with its Head Quarters in Pont Nieppe. Its personnel were a most remarkably fine assortment of the flower of the nation. Except for the basic ration of regular army and reservists, it consisted of officers and men who had quite voluntarily answered the call of the great emergency, many of them from their pioneering roles in remoter parts of the world.

This Armentieres sector of the fighting line in 1915 was an ideal initiation into the grimmer role, which lay ahead of us. Here we learnt what it was to be shot at, and also to perfect that quite subconscious ability of judging whether audible shells in flight were due to drop dangerously close or not. Also there was that ever present necessity of being continuously on the alert when in the face of the enemy.

We were able to acquire that great art of all good artillery officers of keeping opposing lines under perpetual observation, interpreting their dispositions, and preventing any major surprise to our own troops by correctly reading the slightest and every indication of abnormality amongst the enemy. Offensive raids into the German lines were the best of practise in co-operation between all arms, and the serious shortage of field gun ammunition taught care in the method of engaging the variety of targets visible on a normal day. We were also able to apply ourselves on how to contest the inhuman existence of a battle field with its squalor, its lice, its rats and its thousands of other petty beastlinesses.

Mechanisation was then confined to the rear echelons, whereas the fighting troops and their transport were entirely horsed. Every little farmstead had its quota of drivers, living a crowded life in the barn, whilst their very numerous horses were tied out shivering in the raw weather and always knee deep in the seemingly endless mud. Naturally all horses deteriorated badly in the conditions as the wet and cold winter proceeded.

Men's rations were defiantly good, but we had a big surfeit of jam and biscuits, which just went on and on accumulating and this seemed a wicked waste. The base distribution did not allow for finicky distinctions regarding their absorption of their good delivery; we could neither undo nor send back. Rather than condone such waste, we tried it on the horses, who were delighted with this added delicacy to their food, which was generally for the most part lost in the mud. Each one looked forward to his biscuits and jam (favourites and weaklings got two pots) added to their oats and so our horses were in fine order by springtime.

A Battery
112 Brigade RFA
25th Division

My dear Papa,

Just got your letter of first. It has come round to my turn to spend a week up in the observation post. I am sitting up in the gables of a ruined house writing this, and trying to kill Germans at the same time. I have a sergeant here with me watching through a loophole in the wall further down and the telephonist below me by which means we are connected to the Battery and various units around. The telephone system out here is very fine, but the great trouble is that shellfire is continuously cutting the wires.

I am here in this place from when it gets light to when it gets dark, and am about 300 yards from the Bosche trenches. I can watch any movements for miles around; observing is really a most fascinating game, providing there is something doing, but I don't get any exercise. The river behind the Huns is flooding and looks rather as though they have partly evacuated their trenches, as there is no smoke coming from a big strip today. Their communication trenches are flooded for a long way, so they have to use a sort of raised trolley line, which we keep a gun laid on, and they know it too, and when ever they go to and fro they do the whole way at the double; sort of 100 yards sprint and we help them along with a wizz bang now and then.

Like most others I find I have got quite used to the continuous noise of firing, but there is one most annoying thing, and that is, the Huns have a fixed rifle trained on this wall and keep it pretty busy, seldom firing at it at bigger intervals than 2 or three minutes. On the other side they have a machine gun, which lets off every now and then. The Huns seemed to defend their lines very largely by means of machine guns. They do very little firing in the way of artillery at night, except when we attack them, as they are so afraid of us seeing their gun flashes and we have to be very careful for the same reason. There is a high wind blowing today, which makes good shooting very hard, as it is a cross wind, and seems to blow at irregular strength. (Just this moment seen two Bosche going along the aforesaid raised line at the double, so I get a shell after them and knocked the leading one in the water, and the other about turned and went as hard as his legs could carry him, without looking to see how his mate fared). I did not cut down those gum boots; the shop people did as mother and I thought best when we got them, as they are waders. They are very good for battery work, but too short for the trenches; the infantry wear waders for trench work and so do the Huns.

With love from your affectionate son,

Stephen

11th November

C Carver

My dear Godmother,

Thank you for all your gifts. There were so many I won't even try to thank you for them all. We have been much rejoiced lately owing to the arrival of a long expected gramophone, which does tremendous service every evening. Things are really very quiet round here, mostly mine warfare and a certain amount of artillery. The principle enemy here is mud.

We have good stables up at last but the roads seem to get swallowed up as quickly as we build them. Life must be rather alarming with you with these 'Zeppy' times. It is much safer out here with a nice bombproof dugout to sleep in. I hope to get 8 days leave somewhere near Xmas and will try to pay you a flying visit. So many thanks for all your kindness,

Christian

Canon Andrews

By this time we had got a permanent building for the men in time for the winter months. We had no idea how long the conflict would last. People were amazed by the progress Oswin made. Just as the bulk of the work had been down, both Oswin and myself became sick. When a parson is ill it's a bit like a bus man's holiday and I found myself watching from under the bedclothes to see how the various chaplains who visited the sick went about their job – looking out for tips. When I was well enough to move I was sent back to London to get well. I also took a visit to my parents – the first in four years.

Notes taken from Canon's Folly, *page 73.*

18th November

C Carver

My dear Brother,

We are having the very jolliest time here, we have had some ripping snow and now we have got the cutest little fog you ever saw and didn't see through. Things seem to be going badly in the East, what say lad? It seems to me this front is getting a bit of a back number with all the best people going East for the winter this year. We are rather hurt because Fritz hasn't shelled us for over a fortnight. I know he is rather short of ammunition but considering we came all the way from England I think he might take a little interest in us!

What I mean is, is it manners? Pah! Its Hunnish! Carroll and I are now the proud owners of a top-hole gramophone. Any additions to our record collection would be very welcome.

Love to all,

CCC

23rd November

C Carver

My darling Mum,

I am writing this to the strains of 'Bernie the Bomber' this evening before I depart for five days of that infernal sewer life. It will nearly be over by the time you get this, joyful thought. At present my leave is booked for December 25th. We seem to have nothing but these infernal fogs at present. The Venus Waltz is now in full swing. Some top note that!

Well goodnight my very darling mum,

CCC

2nd December

C Carver

My dear Dad,

Thanks much for your letters. I am just back from the old trenches. Everything was frozen hard but dry and clean. The Hun hereabouts is a pretty harmless little creature. He fights by mining, trench mortaring, machine gunning and a little field gunning and sniping. He has deep dugouts and a forest of wire.

When annoyed he waits till evening time and then sends over 8 colossal bombs, which blow out every candle for a mile and are INTENSELY UNPLEASANT. He got 10 months start on us in mining and if we had not taken over from the French would be under our trenches by now. So much for the Hun.

We are just ourselves and bash Fritz about in our usual way. We make a habit of looking over the parapet and bating the opposite number. Fritz does not. Not by any means. We are certainly top dog, a great and wonderful nation, nothing else has any right to exist, and we are bound to win the war. Wouldn't it be awful if I really had a mind like that?

Do you remember that fellow Thorne who took me for English? I have discovered he is the machine gun officer here. What a world! It's a long stride from that quaint army classroom to our next meeting when he brought in what had been his brother and we put him on my bed. However I suppose it is war and in a way its better side.

I hope to get home on the 27th of this month though it is still uncertain. We are pulling down a disused cookhouse this morning and we had the most glorious rat strafe – we must have slain 25 at least. One crowded hour killing the rodent is worth an eternity of fighting Germans. Well I have lots of letters to censor.

Much love from,

CCC

3rd December

Evacuation of Gallipoli begins.

4th December

British land forces in Salonika.

W H Carver

Trench equipment is issued for active service but is then withdrawn and replaced two days later by pith helmets and tropical kit. The 31st Division including the 2 Hull Battalions were sent to Egypt to guard the Suez Canal from a Turkish attack that never came.

Notes taken from The Trench.

15th December

Sir John French resigns. Succeeded by Douglas Haig as Commander in Chief.

25th December

King's Christmas message to troops.

27th December

C Carver
Written by his mother.

Christian arrives home on his first leave looking well and keen to enjoy every minute. His three brothers followed him wherever he went. The first thing he wanted was a hot bath. The holidays now seemed to have begun in earnest. Out came the motor bike and it was wonderful to see him fit back in so well after all he must have seen and been through.

That year a friend of his had brought back from school a ripple of psychic thought – automatic writing. They would collect about a small round table in front of the fire and ask questions. I didn't like their doing it. I shrank from probing into the future even in fun. I dreaded their asking a question the answer to which might have an ill-omened sound. 'Shall I get married?' Christian asked. 'No,' was the reply. (I hated this.) 'Shall I have a rough crossing back to France?' 'Yes,' said the Oracle. He had a smooth one and I cannot tell you how it comforted me.

28th December

Cabinet legislates compulsion – single men before married men.

30th December

Five German mines explode north of Loos causing British casualties.

Alfred Williams

I became Sub Lieutenant and then 1st Lieutenant of the Magnolia. The Captain was a difficult man to please. Everything I did I should have done in another way. The arrival of the first depth charge on the Magnolia was amusing.

The Captain was not wise to new ideas and wanted to mount it up close to the bridge so that he could release it himself. This would have blown up our stern. I argued hotly with him and finally managed to get him to move it to stern.

When it was fitted properly and we had a chance to use it we didn't, due to the Captain being sure we would get a better chance in a minute or so but we never did. After eight months in Magnolia I went for a ten day course on torpedoes in the Vernon, before to going to destroyers. I then joined Satyr at Harwich and Wilson joined Skate. It was nice that we kept together during the war.

In the Skate, no sooner had the Captain handed over command but we were sent out to engage a force of German destroyers and torpedo boats. As we passed one of them our rudder jammed and we went round in circles till we had fixed it. By this time we had sunk the torpedo boat which was much smaller than we were.

Having been sleeping in pyjamas when we were sent out I headed off in them to help pick up survivors in a whaler. At the best of times a whaler can't hold many people beside the crew. We got amongst the prisoners and were helping them onboard when we were recalled as it was felt it wasn't safe to remain off the Dutch coast.

We could not take any more onboard and as we were only twenty yards from the Satyr I told them to swim in that direction and I would return for them. Life belts had been thrown in their direction so I hope they were ok. We could not have taken any more onboard ourselves but next day the Germans accused us of taking in just enough to get information from and leaving the rest to drown. We did all we could and obeyed orders. I got a second DSC for this action, which I always felt uncomfortable with.

1916

4th January

C Carver
Bellevue Farm

My darling Mum,

Well here we are again (as it were). Things have been pretty lively while I have been away. The principle event being a rather triste one I am afraid. Some of the men were taking a German whiz bang shell to pieces in a dug out when a fuse which must have been some kind of high explosive went off. Well one of my best men died and the rest were slightly hurt.

I had a much better crossing this time. We have it direct from Kitchener's secretary that the war will be over this spring. Well, I hope so. I am afraid you may think me unresponsive over my leave. By Jove I did enjoy it! But it is such a precious and necessary thing I don't want to spoil it with sentimentality. As it was I had a thoroughly good time and enjoyed it up to the last minute. Goodnight darling Mum,

From,

Christian

Canon Andrews

It was decided I should head for northern France with the 62nd Division stationed near Newcastle. Once over there I met up with Oswin, which was wonderful. His latest idea was to go to the prisoner of war camps in Germany as their chaplain. Did I want to go too? No I said, the idea was crazy. He reluctantly dropped the idea.

Notes taken from Canon's Folly, *page 75.*

W H Carver

Extract from his letters home.

We are still here awaiting orders (in Port Said) and no news of any mails yet. There are so many things I want to know and the lack of news here is awful. The last of the Brigade are arriving and one of the Battalions had a close shave when a torpedo passed just behind their stern. It has been bitterly cold just recently with gales and sand storms so I have been glad of the extra blankets. We are all getting bored of this place as there is little to do and time hangs heavy but it will be worse when we move further down where there will be no water to waste. The eternal flat sand is so monotonous.

8th January

Evacuation of Gallipoli Peninsula completed. H.M.S. King Edward VII sinks after hitting mine.

12th January

C Carver

My very beloved Mother,

I have joyously tootled out of the trenches this merry morning. Just before I left we had a perfectly gorgeous shoot. Earth, beams, corrugated iron splinters hurtling through the air. Boche retaliated with zeal and put a dozen howitzers into his own wire. Loud applause. Then he got to work with some jolly pretty shrapnel shooting – the best I have seen him do yet. This must all sound very egotistical, Tonnes of love,

Crick

15th January

C Carver

Dearest Mum,

Thanks so much for your letters. The war is going quite all right, rather better than usual since I took charge down here. Lord how heavenly it would be if they transplanted us to a place where there was no mud. By the way I forgot to tell you that I wanted my canvas basin sent out. We have been in action now for very nearly six months and have so far sustained only one casualty. Of course our infantrymen have had a good few more. This warfare is without glamour and excitement.

Every one feels funk when the shells get close. Sometime when you have a vacant moment you could oblige me by sending a card stating whether or not there is any likely hood of us winning this war as the Daily Press leads me to believe there isn't. Things here are much as usual,

Tonnes of love from,

Christian

19th January

W H Carver

My dear Mr Carver,

Thanks very much for your letter and I shall be only too glad to ask for a special thanksgiving in Hessle Church at the morning service on Sunday, for the safe arrival of our 29th Brigade in Egypt. And as you say we do want to be intensely grateful that God has heard our prayers and protected them in this wonderful way on their voyage. Hoping and praying that they may all be protected and returned to us.

I am Yours ever,

Bishop of Hull

24th January

Military Service Bill passed by House of Commons.

C Carver

My darling Mum,

Many thanks for your letters. My mind is a complete blank so I will resume after dinner. Continued after dinner but still feeling unintelligent. I shall probably stay here another week before a spell in the trenches and it seems probable that the Division will move out in the next 3–4 weeks.

Much love to all from,

Christian

27th January

C Carver

My dear Brother,

Many thanks for your letter of the 23rd. So glad school is going well. It's the Kaiser's birthday today, Gott Strafe him for a dirty dog. It seems possible that this Division will be hiked out to the back of behind somewhere pretty shortly. Well cheerio old dear.

Keep cheerful like,

Crick

31st January

Six Zeppelins hit East Anglia and Midlands – 70 dead, 113 injured.

C Carver

My beloved Mum,

Very many thanks indeed for the letters. The question occupying all our thoughts at the moment is gas. I am sure if the wind doesn't change soon there will be some people having a nervous breakdown. We have been losing some trenches due to the use of gas. There has been a rare old dust up last night.

The Germans began by bombarding trenches to the left of our sector. And then every blessed gun in the country got going from about 4.30 to 6.30. They made such a row they quite spoilt my tea and perusal of Punch. It seems quite big changes are shortly pending on the Divisional front. I think our job will change but we will stay here till the end of time. With all this gas about everyone is a bit jumpy. We have had our tube helmets on 6 times in the last 3 days. I will now stop this gassy letter. Well 'roll on the end' as the men say in their letters.

Much love,

Crick

Stephen Williams

Unquestionably it is only the very greatest of mankind who can inspire in battle something more than dutiful discipline, the perfect unquestioned and devotional response at all times, from everyone under his command. With rare personalities it can be almost fanatical because it is occasioned by a total faith in his judgement and leadership as well as mutual fellow sympathy.

One such Battalion Commander came under our support when the 9th Division relived us in February 1916; he was the recently resigned First Lord of the Admiralty, Winston Churchill, and never was a Commanding Officer held in more affectionate respect.

2nd February

C Carver

My dear Dad,

I think we are through the worst of the winter and all the horses are fat and well and are beginning to lose their winter coats so in a month or two they should be looking very fine. The wagon line has been looking better recently too, due to less rain – long may it continue. The Germans have been trying to push south of us about 3 miles south of the Somme. The prevailing easterly wind has ensured plenty of gas alarms some of which were false. I see the old Zepps have been over the Midlands and done some damage in Staffs, I hope it wasn't in our corner of it.

Much love from,

CCC

3rd February

Germans shell Loos.

8th February

Canon Andrews

Not long after my time in France started, I was called upon to help with men who were being shot for desertion. When I was first asked I felt as if out of all the chaplains in France, why did they have to pick on me? I was to tell this prisoner at 7pm that he was to be shot the following morning. I was then to stay with him all night. I would then take the burial service. It was because I had served with the Australians that I was thought best for the job (the man in question being an Aussie). It was an order and however much I wanted to run a mile I summoned up enough courage and entered the cell and found the poor creature sitting on a box. Immediately he stood smartly to attention. He was a regular and had taken part in the famous retreat from Mons. 'I afraid I have come with bad news' I said. Still standing to attention the man replied 'I know sir, you have come to tell me I've got to be shot.' Could anyone ever forget those words or the picture of the soldier standing to attention. Tears ran down my face and I wanted to rush out into the night. Then I wrote lots of letters for him to his mother and various friends. He pulled soiled photos out of his pocket and told me all about them. Every time I looked at my watch I thought it had stopped, so slowly went the time. Would he like me say a prayer? We knelt and I became dumb for minutes on end. What could I say? As the endless night went on, the corporal, about six-foot tall, came in and asked if he would like some refreshments. He said he would like some tea and some buttered toast. In due course the corporal, a gentle creature, came in with the biggest plate of toast I have ever seen, cut thick, partly burnt and covered in butter almost as thick as the toast, out of the kindness of his heart. I sat and watched him eat the lot talking to him all the time by now. For his second cup I dropped in a little morphia, or some other drug the kind doctor had given me. Soon he was fast asleep. While he slept I could hear again the tragic story he had told me. 'I ran away four times and each time they caught me they told me if I ever deserted again I would be shot. My nerve has gone, whatever had happened to me I could not go back to the firing line again.' I so wanted to try and help him escape. Dawn was beginning to break and there was movement outside. The whole camp seemed alive; only my prisoner slept. I left him in the good hands of the corporal and went to talk to the firing party. For them it was the worst job they had had to do. The firing party was waiting, their backs to the prisoner. Suddenly the blindfolded prisoner put up his hand. Could he shake hands with the padre? Slowly I returned. The longest walk of my life, and as the sun was bringing us more light I shook my new friend by the hand, just before he departed. After the funeral service, while the soldiers filled in the grave, the cockney sergeant said cheerfully, 'You know sir, I remember when he was one of the bravest men in the Battalion. He was a very good shot he was.' 'Pity you didn't say that at his court martial,' I replied. 'Never had a chance,' he added. 'Nor had he,' I thought, as I jumped into my waiting car.

Notes taken from Canon's Folly, *page 79.*

C Carver

My dear Dad,

Sounds like some raid but I think it extremely unlikely they will try anything like that again with as much success. Still I don't like the idea of the war penetrating my native home. I bade farewell to D3 on Monday and am now in a permanently reinforcing position and only fire seriously in emergencies.

Much love from,

CCC

11th February

H.M.S. Arethusa mined off east coast.

H M Wilson
HMS Euryalus

My dear Mother,

When I got back the other day I got all your letters. I can't believe Charlie has been killed. I am hoping for some leave soon but it depends on what the Turks do.

Your loving son,

Hubert.

23rd February

C Carver

My dear Dad,

We had a rare old strafe yesterday. I think the Boschs where fed up with our mining and it must have been worrying them so they decided to do some dirty doings on the old tambo.

We responded heartily and they shoved back in a hurry. Some of them however stayed with us. The landscape is now snow clad and the temperature is low. I saw the French bring down a Zepp in the south. Well done them. The men are all full of beans which they vent on a football during the lunch hour.

Well much love from,

Crick

29th February

C Carver

My dear Mother,

We have been having the same old beastly weather. The snow is becoming our worst enemy as thawing does more damage to the trenches than any German shell. I was rather amused by a small dog's antics this morning that was rushing about outside our trenches when they were being lightly shelled by whiz bangs.

I have never seen such appallingly bad shooting in my life. But good or bad he didn't care a button for shells and rushed up to each one as it burst with great enthusiasm. They eventually put one about 2 feet away from him but beyond knocking him over he didn't seem to mind it at all it fact it rather quickened his interest. I wish we were all like that, so I do.

I am afraid we get a lot more credit for enduring the hardships than we deserve. By us I mean the gunners. The infantry have a mouldy time in the trenches. Everyone else has a comfortable time although dull. We through no merit of our own take part in everything but far enough back to live in comfort.

Today we had time to finish our tea in comfort before letting off 175 rounds in time for dinner. I must break off now to write the operation report.

Tonnes of love,

CCC

Stephen Williams

In March the 25th Division took over the Vimy Ridge Sector, north of Arras, then held by a French Colonial Division. Their filthy trench existence and lack of sanitation beggars description. Our guns were in a very exposed position and constantly shot at near the Souchez road, with a rear observation post, for ground control, in one of the road trees, and forward O.P.'s in the front line. The tree was a perfect copy of the original one which, one night was cut down and removed and this hollow steel lined one grew simultaneously in its place, and remained undetected until May when it forgot to grow any leaves!

The sector was the scene of some of the intense form of trench warfare: guns, trench mortars, rifle and hand grenades, sniping, bombing saps, listening posts, night fighting patrols were all ceaselessly active. At dawn and at twilight there was always an uncanny silence, a most intense and impressive silence, whilst both sides were on the alert to anticipate possible exploding of enemy underground mines. Tunnelling so as to blow up big underground charges under one another's trench system was quite thrilling in its way as one could plainly hear, when underground, the enemy doing the same thing in other saps around one!

Danger was 'smelt' when silence prevailed since this indicated the completion of their task, the readiness in their galleries, and blowing with probable entombment, was imminent. Immediately a mine was 'put up' all guns threw a screen beyond it to prevent the enemy reinforcing the hand to hand fight to secure the lip of the new crater. The power of the explosion of the bigger mines was often so terrific that it momentarily numbed the limbs of those nearby, and it frequently caused minor disorganisation by partial burials through trenches collapsing. The far lip was vital to secure because of the important new observation, but as so often happened both sides only managed to secured their side of the crater and no material profit was made. The Vimy Ridge was a great test of morale. The regiments of fine offensive and co-operative spirit, always ready to seize the initiative, suffered the loss of much smaller numbers killed and wounded than did the units of low morale whose defensive covering attitude brought on themselves additional casualties as well as many cases of nervous derangement, then called shell shock.

2nd March

C Carver

Dear Mother,

I address you thus briefly because my stock of humorous opening is nearly expended. I am writing this seating on a packing case due to our chairs being packed away in readiness to our move to the back tomorrow. We seem to know the landscape here so well and all the familiar landmarks seem like old friends now that its time to leave them. After a 6 month duration we are moving back with only 2 or 3 casualties. I wonder where we shall come into action next. Well we are about to partake so I will close here. We are going where *drains are of unusually rancid species, an idiotic remark, which has significance, largely pristine.

Much love,

Crick

**What he had been trying to tell them was that he was close to DAOURS.*

5th March

Zeppelin raids on East and Northeast Counties. 18 killed, 52 injured.

6th March

Women's National Land Service Corps inaugurated.

C Carver

My darling Mum,

I am writing this in my billet at 11.45pm so don't expect any scintillation. We successfully moved out from the firing line after dark on Friday evening. After breakfast the following morning we continued on in the snow and the conditions were the most miserable we have struck yet. It snowed all of the 12 miles march. We have got a top-hole mess. Griffin and Carroll went into Arras today and came back with a large amount of supplies – our mess bill will be huge. Well it's past 12 so a very good night to you,

CCC

H M Wilson
HMS Euryalus

My dear Mother,

We got sent up to the front line trenches on the east bank of the canal the other day. They sent about 100 men up altogether. We were split up and I went to the 6th Brigade with about 25 men. We were there for two nights but no one knew quite what for. I enjoyed it very much and so did the men. We had rotten weather unfortunately with partial sandstorms the whole time. Everything you eat and drink is full of sand. I wouldn't be a soldier – too uncomfortable and the desert is no joke. We shall be having Zepps all over the country now. I was surprised they got to Bath but I don't think they are worth stopping as they do very little damage. I expect we shall be in whites soon and I should be home in August. There is no other news at the moment.

Your loving son,

Hubert

12th March

C Carver

My darling Mum,

It has been a lovely day here today and we have much enjoyed ourselves. We had a brigade church parade attended in force by the officers. Quite a good little service it was. I have been out riding this afternoon. Well pretty shortly we shall return to our first love, there we shall enjoy the unique position of extreme right of the British Army in France and guardians of the gate of the Somme. Well I think that is all for the moment.

Very much love from,

Christian

16th March

C Carver

My darling Mum,

Thanks so much for all your letters. Chances of leave are very much below par. To be exact all leave has been stopped and it's hard to say when it will start again. Well think of us going into harness again next Monday. Everyone seems to be in a state of wind-up about it. However, come what may our little stay down here has been very pleasant. Socks are top-hole,

Love to all,

Crick

17th March

Food prices rise 48% in Great Britain.

18th March

Allied bomb Zeebrugge. Royal Defence Corps formed.

C Carver

Dearest Mum,

And here we are again. The other side of the valley this time on a nice road under some trees. We have good deep French made dugouts and I must say it is a delightful little corner of the war with good views all round. But the whole place is pitted with shell holes mostly from the Fritz show. We wend our way through the wood and prudently hide behind trees as some shells keep falling in the near vicinity. 200 feet below us is a village and the river and the view along this seems to stretch forever. One day when this is all over the view will be worth another look. What say you? Leave has reopened so I should get some at the end of May or early June.

Much love,

Christian

30th March

C Carver

My dear Dad,

Thanks for your letters. I spend my days very pleasantly here. I dine, sleep and breakfast with the East Surreys and spend my days in an observing station on the top of a cliff. Below is a small hamlet, then comes the river, then a sort of no mans land peninsular enclosed by a loop of the river and then the German side of the loop. To the left is the small village of C where some of the fighting has been recently. There are very few trenches so you can often catch the Hun in the open. Well for this child, bed.

Much love from,

Christian

3rd April

C Carver

My dear Brother,

I am writing this in a trench that is also serving as an observation post. It's a nuisance not being able to get a leave this holiday but this show at Verdun was to blame as we had to take over a lot of line up north to relieve the French. This is absolutely the spot to be in this war at least if you're a gunner. Things here are rather quiet touch wood though I am sure the Bosch has got something up his sleeve.

Love from,

C

5th April

Military Medal instituted.

7th April

C Carver

Dear Brother,

'Tis a Picardy Spring
The bluebells and primroses show it
(And also my fancy takes wing)
By violets and such you may know it
There are thrushes and robins and tits
Wrens, thrushes a few, also blackbirds,
And each unconcernedly sits
Expanding its little throat skywards.
But I could enjoy the spring more
Without all these shells and trench mortars
Bombs, snipers and whiz bangs galore
(That last couple jolly near caught us)
Enough of this cynical slop
I can see some fat Boschs in Frise
This bilge-water burbling must stop
Whilst I snipe them with consummate ease.
I missed them (I usually do)
Unfortunate that the day is a mist 'un
I must now have a shot at a Curlu
So goodbye and good luck
From yours,
Christian

11th April

German losses since start of war are 2,730,917.

15th April

C Carver

Dearest Mum,

There seem to be more civilians appearing every day. I counted seven women one old man and two children at one moment this morning. So the real attack at Verdun is only just commencing as up to now we have only seen little skirmishes. 'Wind up,' is the new expression used by the BEF. It signifies alarm and terror. Dud is also a new one for anything that doesn't come off. You will be pleased to hear we have just repulsed six Germans. I had an amusing day shooting today. The Hun in Frise doesn't know he's being watched from here and his misplaced caution when he is in full view is very funny. I saw all sorts. Clean Huns, dirty Huns, some with jumpers on. They will have tales to tell of their narrow escape this afternoon if they ever make it back to the fatherland.

The Huns have been shelling this sector with exasperating energy these last couple of days until the Surreys put up a sign, which read... 'If you will persist in this behaviour we shall be compelled to fire our rifle grenade,' to which Fritz replied, 'sorry,' and thereupon desisted.

Tonnes of love,

Christian

17th April

C Carver
Doggerel Dodderings on VI Sector

Of all the towns of France	
Are none more fair than…	*Vaux*
Have you finished with the world	
If from every urban whirl you	
Turn with loathing then lie curled	
'Neath the carriere at …..	*Curlu*
If you want to take your ease	
None more suitable than …	*Frise*
Are you blasé, bloated, bored?	
Angry passions hard to stem?	
Then when we've laid down the sword	
Go at once and visit……..	*Hem*
If you're hard up, worn or sad	
If your spirit's faint and weary	
Then of course my simple lad	
You must go and stay at ………	*Clery*
And you'll like it more and more	
When you go to ……	*Maricourt*
Are your amours played upon	
Has your heart been badly bent in	
Try a journey to …….	*Peronne*
Or better still to Mont St. Quentin	
Are you tired of lust of gain	
Bills and bank notes, bonds and money	
You will find at Haut………	*Allaines*
That the outlook's always sunny	
If you are clever then perhaps	
You will fill up all these gaps	

CCC

19th April

H M Wilson

My dear Father,

Mother told me you had arrived safely though you were attacked after you left Malta. Williams is in the Magnolia and has got some leave and I am hoping for some too as I have been away for nearly two and a half years. Everything goes on much the same out here.

Your affectionate son,

Hubert

H M Wilson

My dear Mother,

Please thank Patricia for the cake, which I am afraid, must have been sunk. We are very much amused at the new American note. I don't think America can risk going to war with Germany.

It is a most extraordinary state of affairs. We are all wondering when the great offensive is coming. I think Verdun has put it off a bit but the Germans cannot be in a position to resist a really big offensive on our part if they continue these sacrifices.

I don't think any of the homeward bound letters have been sunk lately so you should get about one a week from me.

Your loving son,

Hubert

25th April

C Carver

My darling Mum,

This is to let you know that as things are at present, I shall roll in some time on May 3rd so don't let M and H go back to school.

Much love from,

Crick

26th April

H M Wilson
HMS Euryalus

My dear Mother,

We got in yesterday, the anniversary of the landing. Williams, who is my greatest friend out here, is going home.

His brother who has a lot to do with the big people at the Admiralty managed to get it worked. So many people I know seem to have got home but I am still hard at it after 2 and 1/2 years.

Your loving son.

Hubert

27th April

John Williams's ship, H.M.S. Russell, is mined in Mediterranean, 124 lost.

Extract from the inquiry/court-martial over sinking of HMS Russell.

Sir,

I regret to report the following:

On the morning of Thursday 27th of April 1916, HMS Russell was proceeding towards the Grand Harbour, Malta. At 5.37am while the ship was on a steady course and one mile off 'C' channel, I observed a violent explosion on the port side aft, abreast the Ward Room hatch and shortly afterwards another explosion of the same sort a little further forward. I gave the orders, 'Stop both engines, close watertight doors and clear lower deck,' and shortly after, 'out boats.'

It appeared to me that the explosion took place a considerable distance under water and the ship immediately took a slight list to port, which gradually increased but not any very great extent at first. Signals were made to Castle, 'Have been struck by mine or torpedo. Send tug immediately.'

Observing that the ship was badly on fire aft, I ordered the engine room, 'flood aft magazines,' and later, 'flood starboard foremost wing compartments,' with a view to correcting the list. As the ship showed no immediate signs of sinking I ordered, 'Half speed ahead' with a view to beaching her, but as the order was not at once obeyed I had to send the message again, via Mr Westall, midshipman. I then observed a third explosion not as violent as the first two, which apparently took place in the aft turret blowing off the canvas cover and the left sighting hood.

Meanwhile both cutters had been lowered, the sailing pinnace hoisted out and both carley rafts and both cask rafts, which were stowed on the quarterdeck, were launched. Mr Westall returned to report that owing to the fires he was unable to get near the starboard engine room.

HMS Harrier had now closed on us and as we were listing heavily I ordered, 'fall in on the forecastle.' The fire was gaining rapidly and I was worried the magazines might start exploding at any minute.

HMS Harrier was now coming alongside but we ordered her not to as we were about to capsize and this would have seriously damaged her. I ordered all hands to go overboard and make for the nearest vessel. Just after I left the ship she rolled over and remained bottom up for a short time and then sank by the stern.

In my opinion two mines struck the ship. To the best of my belief there was no one still alive remaining on the ship when she went down and I attribute the loss of life to the two explosions and to effect of the fumes.

All the wounded found were got away on rafts or boats. Those books in use on the bridge I personally put in a specially constructed weighted wallet just before I left the bridge to ensure sinking.

I have the honour to be, Sir, your obedient servant

William Bowden Smith

(Captain)

Extract taken from records at The National Archives, Public Records Office ADM1/8455/97

30th April

C Carver

My dearest Mum,

Careful investigation reveals the fact that I arrive in England on the 4th. I am having a pleasant life here and the weather is glorious.

Love from,

CCC

4th May

C Carver

Christian arrives home in the early afternoon. The time that followed was spent in the usual happy way with the added bonus of lighter evenings allowing them all to enjoy each others company for longer. I sat and chatted with him most evenings after the others had gone to bed. He was turning into such a fine man and my worries that trench life would spoil him eased. He caught the mid-day train to Paddington on May 13th.

5th May

H M Wilson

My dear Mother,

Patricia's cake has finally arrived, quite fresh and very good. Please thank her for me. Williams' brother was on HMS Russell, that was torpedoed, and we don't know yet whether he was picked up. About 60 of the officers were saved. He has already lost one brother at Loos and the news about the Russell is even more sickening.

Your loving son,

Hubert

As yet my grandfather didn't know whether he had lost a second brother in the war.

14th May

C Carver

Dearest Mum,

Behold me returned. The journey back was a good one. We are about to undergo a strenuous course of training so I must go and get to work on it.

Much love,

Crick

16th May

Military Service Bill passed in House of Commons – extending compulsion to married men.

C Carver

My dear Dad,

So sorry for not writing sooner but on my return I found everyone very short-handed. I have just been up in a plane for the first time. Some sensation. Rather fascinating but I shouldn't care to do it for a living.

Love to all from,

Crick

17th May

Daylight Saving Bill passed.

W H Carver

We are recovering from our trench tour in an ideal spot. The weather has turned lovely again and we are in a large wood in hut shelters and tents under enormous beech and oak trees and it is really quite beautiful and with the full moon at night – quite romantic too. Only the thunder of the guns in front reminds us of what is going on.

The battalion that relieved us had a rough time so altogether we were fortunate though we did catch the rain, which is equal in beastliness to shelling. We are painting our tents to make them less visible. Discipline is strict out here, as it should be.

Our band is playing again in preparation for a party under the trees tomorrow evening. The Brigade General has died from spotted fever which is very sad.

19th May

W H Carver

We hear peace rumours and I see the papers are talking of it. I do wish it was all over as the strain of it all is so very great.

20th May

C Carver

Dearest Mum,

Horrors! I do believe it's been a week since I last wrote. I really feel I have lived this week. Tomorrow I am off to the Front on a motor lorry and my job will be digging this new position place. It should be rather jolly as Caroll has just returned again. One can get a certain amount of enjoyment out of the Front when not engaged in actual hostilities. You are in touch with everything but not responsible for holding the wretched thing. You have no idea what miserably ineffective looking obstacles the trenches appear from a plane. Deceptive, one has to be careful about these things.

Much love to all from,

Crick

21st May

W H Carver

We had an open-air concert in the wood last night and it was a great success and all passed off well. The men's voices sounded grand. The last post was sounded and we also sang Abide With Me. Today being Sunday we have not worked so hard and had a parade service under the trees – the first since Egypt.

I expect to leave this wood on the 24th and go into the village we were in before. Five days there and we should then see us back at the Front. Holy Communion was received by around 50 men in well war-worn uniforms with the sound of the guns clearly heard in the background.

23rd May

W H Carver

We move into our village tomorrow and will miss our lovely wood. Last night the Battalion went up to dig trenches, which is always hard work in the dark. There was also a strafe going on at the same time but we were a little bit back so had a nice view of the show. It is wonderful to see shells and shrapnel bursting at night.

25th May

C Carver

My dear Dad,

I am now at the Front again in charge of the digging of our latest position. I shall be here for a fortnight or so. It's the usual thing, flowers blooming, guns booming, nightingales singing, shells shrieking. Someone forgot our kit when we came up this morning and by the time they arrived it was raining hard so they were of little comfort.

Before we had been here an hour, boom-woa-bang right over our heads. Two colossal 5.9s crumped 10 yards in front of the position and nearly frightened the life out of me. We feel frightfully cut off here with no telephone or transport. Our neighbours are no help at all, as all they try to do is pinch our stuff.

Well cheerio,

Crick

H M Wilson

My dear Mother,

We have now left the Persian Gulf and have gone south back to civilisation. We ought to have quite a decent time ahead of us. The Captain told Williams and me we ought to wear our ribbons. When the monsoon breaks in June it will be much cooler. Awful bad luck, Williams did lose his brother John when the Russell was torpedoed. It's the second he has lost in the war now. An awful loss for him. I suppose the mine exploded under the gunroom. I do hope I get through all right. I don't think there is any more news.

Your loving son,

Hubert

My grandfather had now lost his two older brothers in the war. We have no record of when exactly his family had been informed.

28th May

C Carver

Dear Brother,

There's a nasty horrid battle going on outside as I write this. All sorts of stuff hurtling about. I don't know what can have happened unless the Hun got his ammunition allowance yesterday or maybe its someone's birthday. They'll get the opposite soon if they aren't careful. The worst of it is that they have goaded the Battery behind us who are now firing right through us with deafening effect. In another few minutes I shall go and fish out my gas helmet. I will. I am absolutely trembling with fright. Steady my lad, remember you come from Birmingham. That's better. This is where we pause for dinner. First soup, gargle splash, then salmon chased with a lump of bread, steak, beans, potato, mhm, tchah, mhm. Peaches from a goodly tin, plop slither, Yours,

Crick

1st June

Stephen Williams

In June 1916 the 25th Division was withdrawn from the Vimy Ridge and moved southwards as a reserve for the Battle of the Somme, due to open on 1st of July. We gunners lay up west of Aveluy Wood, where the cavalry corps took such a pounding in the German counter preparation from their Thiepval position. To our south was plainly visible the gilded idol on the top of the Albert Cathedral, so curiously suspended in the peculiar accident of shellfire. It was in constant view of a large section of the contending forces and every soldier, British and French, said no decision would be reached in the war until it had finally crashed. Later we found that German prisoners volunteered that they held just the same idea. I believe that it eventually fell in the late summer of 1918! The failure of the opening phase of the battle put us into action between the river Ancre and Orvilliers-la-Boisselle. Our attacking lines of infantry had been mown down before reaching the German lines and were a dreadful spectacle. Additional to our work of trying to maintain the general attack, the recovery of the wounded lying in the shell holes of 'no mans land' was a difficult diversion and took days. Many of their wounds in the hot weather of the time became a mass of fly maggots. This, our doctors claimed, actually saved a great many.

Official histories can recall better than we wish to remember about the terrific struggle with the Thiepval area, and later amongst the woods to the south of the Bapaume Road, but one of the most striking performances was the taking of Pozieres by the Australians. It was the most heartening after a series of dreadful failures. There was one thing most galling about the Aussies. They cleaned us out of our best riding horses, whilst we were fighting our guns in the line. Our whole brigade of horses were tethered 'textbook fashion' near Albert, with the officers chargers pegged out independently at the top end of the series of section lines.

The officers' horses included some exceptionally good hunters, and private horses, which for affectionate reasons they had managed to get allowed to accompany them to the war. One dark night a lot of Australian rowdies purpose-fully occupied the attention of all the pickets at the bottom end of the lines. After quelling this, the whole of the officer's horses, not then on duty, were gone. Not one of them was ever recovered; no doubt hogging, docking and discolouring quickly altered their appearances. There was something greatly to be admired about all the many gallant colonial troops whose homes were not directly threatened by war, but had come forward voluntarily prepared to die in our nation's defence. It was a most touching thing to be later on lying in a bad in Etaples Base Hospital between two terribly wounded, and dying officers, very far from those they cherished.

As twilight set in, one of them quietly succumbed, whilst the other in his delirious agonies, continued to let out the most piercing cries. At 10pm he gave his last gasp and then most curiously a bugler in an adjoining camp sounded 'lights out' and there was an ominous silence everywhere. My boyish mind in spite of the multitude of horrors it had experienced, was most deeply impressed.

After discharge from hospital in England, everyone was sent, whilst convalescing, to one of the numerous reserve depots. Frome in Somerset was a delightful enough place but there were several officers there, as in any such depot, who took the greatest care to make themselves so indispensable that they would not be sent to share the risk of fighting again. Associating with these creatures rankled badly with any who had a high sense of duty ingrained so we repeatedly applied to be sent back to France. Probably our families would have been much annoyed if they had known of this inspiration and the wit it entailed. When pressing this application, none of us could foresee how well or badly we were likely to stand up to shellfire on re-acquaintance and to this day it is always a matter of wonder.

5th June

H.M.S. Hampshire bombed off Scottish coast. Lord Kitchener and staff drowned.

7th June

C Carver

My dear Brother,

Yes I have been flying. I have been packed off to study the question of co-operation between aircraft and artillery. The observer sits just behind the engine and the pilot is just behind him. The pilot controls the rudder with his feet. The plane has a wireless, which is just a drum of wire let out in the air to trail behind. Sending only as no method of receiving has been invented yet. By means of ground signals (strips of canvas) they can let the pilot know when they are ready to fire.

Once they have fired he can then correct their shots. Once the skids are pulled away the pilot opens her out and, after about 200 yards you feel her leave the ground and mother earth sinks away to the proportions of a map in a few minutes. The pilot then heads her for the line and it takes us 10 minutes to cover the 16 miles. Before one can see our fighting history all laid out. As you get near the line the pilot turns and you cling on frantically and pray hard that the earth will stop whirling round and round. Stop! Stop a minute! This is getting too much for me.

Having been completely flattened out by the naval scrap, Verdun, Ypres and a few other brain cracking events, I have just heard that Kitchener, Robertson and staff have all gone down in the Hampshire on their way to Russia. Look here, I thought we were supposed to be winning this war. Here and all along the line are the armies, which bear his name.

Yours truly,

Crick

8th June

Compulsion replaces voluntary enlistment in Great Britain.

H M Wilson

My dear Father,

We left Bombay last night. We have had a fortnight there and it's not a bad place though we were there at the hottest time. Still it was a great improvement on the Gulf. The fight in the North Sea seems to have turned out very well for us. One can't feel very joyful about it though losing so many officers. I knew a good many of them too. A naval scrap isn't a joke by any means nowadays, as the shell fumes seem to be very bad. There is some chance of us coming back to Egypt about September or October I think. We heard just before we sailed last night that Lord Kitchener went down in the Hampshire. Who do you think will take his place? It makes one rather pessimistic about the duration of the war. The wind is getting up now and I don't think there is any other news to report.

Your loving son,

Hubert

14th June

C Carver

Dearest Mum,

Just a scrawl in absolutely frantic haste. We have been so full up with work we can hardly breathe. Ironic having got nothing for a fortnight. The weather is and has been perfectly appalling. Rain, rain, and rain day after day. The valley is in a shocking state. Great doings are planned but I cannot say any more other than I may be a poor correspondent for the next week or so. Sorry I must be so repressive with news but one cannot say much so better nothing at all, which cannot be then misunderstood. Much love to Dad and all,

Crick

17th June

H M Wilson

My dear Mother,

I do hope some of my letters are getting through. Thanks so much for yours. We left Colombo yesterday. There was a memorial service for Lord Kitchener while we were there. The Russian advance is good work and if it can be maintained should produce important results. I think it is directly due to the naval fight off Jutland.

Your loving son,

Hubert

25th June

Preliminary British bombardment along Somme Front and northwards.

H M Wilson

My dear Mother,

Since I last wrote we have been to Penang. We left yesterday but it wasn't a very interesting sort of a place. We shan't go any further east than this I think. We should get mails soon and a report on the Jutland action. My final exams start tomorrow and last 2 and a half-days so it will be a relief when they are all over. No other news really,

Your loving son,

Hubert

26th June

W H Carver in a letter to his wife

We have been in these trenches since the 23rd. We have had an active time but the papers will tell you more about it than I will be able. The mess is all very awful and the continual bombarding is tiring. I am hoping to get out tonight for a short time. We all need a rest but this time it is not to be. It has poured with rain as usual and the trenches are dreadful again. We get water up in petrol tins so tea tastes of petrol. It's not bad however when it's the only thing you can get. We have lost quite a few officers some of them very new. If you could only see us covered in mud and dirt. I would now be glad of an hour or two back in Egypt. We are so tired and long so much for peace. I suppose if it wasn't for the shells, being out of doors so much would be a healthy life. Thank God I keep well and have some protection. I will appreciate every daily thing that I think mundane when I return. I have so much to say that would be so interesting but I must not say it!

30th June

Continued Allied bombardment on Western Front.

C Carver

Dearest Mum,

You will have gathered from your daily paper that things are doing all along the Western Front. We ain't 'alf into it neither. Proper show it is. The old Hun has got his tail down badly this time for which I can't blame him. There is still a certain amount of life in his artillery, which is rather annoying, but we have made him show his hand. Poor old Bosche. A good many scores are going to be settled with him before too long.

Well good luck to me. I hope I get through this all right. The continual stare of death and mud around one is apt to making one quite depressed. That is nothing however to what the private soldier has to go through without a grumble and I have come to the conclusion that he is the most wonderful man I have ever met. He wades through miles of mud, eats it, sleeps in it on the fire step, sees people to the left and right of him blown to pieces and yet he never murmurs.

Well we're off soon so wish us luck. Our far-flung battle line is thundering and so forth. We got it pretty bad on the nights of the 20th and 21st but he is getting his reward now.

Love to all from,

Christian

1st July

Great Franco-British offensive begins on 25-mile front north and south of Somme.

2nd July

C Carver

Dearest Mum,

Well we have made our little bit of history I think. After 7 days solid shooting we kicked off yesterday and got our objective i.e. the west end of M-n village. Everyone was wonderfully good and lucky too as they met with little resistance and got into the village with out a hitch. The Surreys who I was liasing with got badly cut up but did get there in the end. Only four of their twenty officers got through.

I moved up to the trenches on the afternoon of the 30th and yesterday morning after an intense bombardment the infantry pushed. Not knowing quite what to shell the Hun temporised by shelling this dugout all day. I have never thirsted for anyone's blood like I did then. I spent the day linking up the infantry with the artillery.

Today I have been exploring some of the captured front and support trenches. I picked this card up in a Bosche trench that I have just been to look at. Rather a horrid site it was. The Bosche are mostly dead in their trenches while our men are dead outside. We got a lot of prisoners, which is a goodly site. How on earth the infantry did it I don't know. Absolutely wonderful show from beginning to end. But my, it was some battle yesterday, one of the world's greatest I suppose and the old Division has proved its worth. But I have lost so many good friends though and from what one can see the Bosche died fighting and he appears to have manned his parapet fairly strongly. As liaison officer between the infantry and artillery I heard everything that happened. Jolly interesting.

Love to all,

Crick

W H Carver

I am now for the moment back in the old village having had quite a 10-day spell. We were in the trenches all that time during which there was incessant bombardment. We escaped most of the hard fighting on the 1st as we were in reserve trenches behind the front line and rather on the side of a hill so could see this wonderful, fearful and awful sight and awful smoke and din of battle. We are holding ourselves ready on an hour's notice to move again so we are sleeping all we can. I hadn't had my boots and cloths off at all during those 10 days and was totally caked in clay and mud, unshaven and dirty. I am so tired of it all and long for it to end. I have lost so many friends in this Division due to the last skirmish.

4th July

Heavy thunderstorms impede operations.

5th July

British improve position between Somme and Ancre. Slight advance in other sectors.

6th July

British win ground on slopes of Thiepval. Lloyd George made Secretary of State for War.

W H Carver

After many contradicting orders we have now moved right out of the trenches. All is joy and peace. The Division is refitting after the battle. It's amazing. Having spent the last three months in the trenches I can hardly believe it. No guns to be heard, no mud. We should stay here for around 2 weeks by which time the line should be broken so trench warfare will be over. I won't mind being sent to the Front so much. We feel like a lot of jolly schoolboys. Houses aren't blown to pieces, there are no shell holes and the gardens have flowers in them! There is no leave expected for us soon as there is still much to be accomplished but great satisfaction is expressed by all the higher authorities, as I am sure you will read in the papers.

7th July

Congratulatory message to troops from King George.

C Carver

My dear Dad,

I shall never forget my 19th birthday but I do hope future ones are spent in not quite the same manner. The show on the 1st had been proceeded by 7-day continual bombardment. There absolutely couldn't be any hell worse than what went on. On the night of the 30th we came into position.

My job was liaison officer. I was installed in a jolly hefty little dugout just behind the front line where I was connected by phone to Battalion Head Quarters just across the trench and also to the infantry and Griffin in the rear who had a topping view of the whole show. The night was quiet except for the odd shell playing over the assembly trenches. I managed to get a good cup of tea at 5.30, which was diluted with plenty of rum. Pearce and Neville came in both radiant and delayed everything for the best. After the rum I felt ready to go right through and shake hands with the Russians.

We got to battle stations and the final intense bombardment commenced. The noise was terrific and the eardrums suffered terribly. Needless to say our wire was cut pretty shortly and people had to go out under fire to mend it. Two were buried while doing this.

Zero hour arrived and we heard a wild cheer above the continuous roar and the East Surreys were on their way to get their own back. Reports started coming in which I passed on. They were mainly that the Germans were holding out.

The Surreys won through to the village after a very violent scrap. Neville and Pearce were both killed. The rest of the day was spent in consolidation. I went up in the plane today for observation and saw a wave of little figures washing over the Bosche trenches while they were getting hell from the Hun's big stuff. However they got the remains of the village,

Much love to all,

Crick

H M Wilson

My dear Mother,

We have passed our exams so you can now address my letters Sub Lieut. H Wilson. I have been appointed to the Mallow. Events have moved frightfully quickly the last few days. We finished exams and were immediately told to leave ship. We thought this might be to go home but it isn't to be. I don't know when I shall be home.

Your loving son,

Hubert

11th July

C Carver

Dearest Mum,

On the 8th we got orders to move out and I was quite reluctant to after all the awful things I had seen, as strange as that may sound. However a gas shell landed just as we were about to leave so this hurried me along. I slipped up and down the side of a hill in my box respirator and attended an expiring man. I might have been upset before 'The Somme' but such things now appear quite minor details. We are now about 7 miles from the Front and loving every minute of the peace and restful time.

Heaps of love,

Christian

14th July

End of first phase of Battle of the Somme.

19th July

C Carver

Dearest Mum and all,

Our delightful week has come to an abrupt end with an order to come into action at once. And about 2 fi yards from the Hun front line. The position had never been occupied and the only cover was about 3 feet deep. Just as we had got settled the Huns put a salvo of 4 right into us. We will draw a veil over the next fi an hour.

Capt. Wager died, as did a few others. Many were hit and we lost 15 horses. I was standing alongside one of them; the man on the horse was killed, as was the man just behind me and also poor Wagor who was a few yards away. I got him into the trench and did what I could but he died later in the dressing station.

Three hours later once things were sorted we came into action again at the same place! We spent the evening digging ourselves in and were shelled hard the following morning. A fellow called Patterson came to take command so I left leaving Carroll for which I felt dreadful but orders is orders. I spent the rest of the day looking after the poor old horses. Don't worry about me mum, things are improving and this child will get through all right. I won't need to fear much after this. Well heaps of love to all from,

Crick

20th July

Battle in Longueval and Delville Wood continues.

23rd July

Second phase of Somme battle begins.

24th July

C Carver

Dearest Mum,

Shortly after I wrote to you last I heard a rumour that we were being withdrawn. This turned out to be correct but not before our trench had been shelled and buried 12 men. 2 were killed and the rest were shaken but the worst of it was that the five men who helped dig them out all got killed by shrapnel. One of them was the best man I had got. We spent the night under canvas and said a long farewell to Picardy where we have fought for the last year. Carroll and I had a good confab about the last year and recollected the jolly good times and the times when we were so very lucky. Well absolutely the best to everyone,

From,

Crick

PS chance of leave v. remote in fact negligible.

28th July

British capture Delville Wood and Longueval village.

29th July

Activity south of Ypres and in Loos salient.

C Carver

My dear Dad,

Well here we are in Flanders about 15 miles from the line and the Belgian Boarder and about 10 miles from Wipers. Thank the Lord we are well away from the Somme. We had a good journey up via the seacoast. The views are pleasing but not impressive. We shall probably be in action within the week. I have reached the state of not caring a blow what happens. Things are good at the moment but not expected to last.

Much Love,

Christian

1st August

C Carver

Dearest Mum,

We will be leaving this place soon and it is a cause of much regret to us. But I believe we are going into a quieter bit of line. I hope so, as we feel efficient but unpushful. We are always prepared to biff Huns but prefer to do it in comfort. Well good night to you all, love,

Crick

11th August

H M Wilson

My dear Mother,

I arrived on the Mallow about 5 days ago and so far I like my job very much. It is nice to have responsibility and to decide things and to see the result of your efforts as second in command.

I am practically in charge of the fighting efficiency of the ship. There are a tremendous lot of improvements I intend to make in time. Not much more news at present.

Your loving son,

Hubert

13th August

W H Carver

I am just preparing to be moved off to a hospital. I have had a temperature of 103 on me for three or four days now and had hoped to shake it off but at last I have been made to give in. I was unable to inspect the front line today. Many of us have got it here. Sometimes it's called trench fever. I hope it will not turn into measles, which it has in some cases.

The motor ambulance is coming for me as close as it can get to the front line. I feel rather awful that I have escaped wounds all these months and then have to give in to a temperature – yes I do feel awful. They think I should be right in about ten days. I do feel so rotten and they carry me on a stretcher and won't let me dress myself.

15th August

King returns from a visit to Armies on Western Front.

C Carver

Dearest Mum,

Thanks for the cake. There is absolutely no news here except just between us and Fritz don't you know. We have a wonderful neighbourhood on both sides of us who try to help in every way and are a great example of carrying on. The flat country that we are in now though is a beast.

Much love to all from,

C

W H Carver

I am here at the field hospital a little way back from the line. The hours seem so long. I am in an Officer's ward with 25 others, most of which are recovering from trench fever. My temperature still won't drop below 101 and I am beginning to feel like an old man. It's all so depressing.

17th August

Violent artillery fighting north and south of the Somme.

W H Carver to his wife
No 7 Stationing Hospital Boulogne.

I was brought in here last night. The hospital seems extremely well arranged. It takes about 500 patients. After the journey I had a long night's sleep and am feeling a little better. But just so so weak. There are lots of trench fever sufferers here too and I am told I will be kept here for a week maybe two. Then 3 weeks leave in England but it all depends if I can get rid of the fever/ temperature. I can look out over the sea when it's clear and imagine I can see dear old Blighty. When I get the leave I must make every minute count with you all as we are set for a long winter campaign.

This hospital was a hotel about to open just before the war began. So it makes a very convenient hospital being near everything and more importantly the ships to take the injured back to old Blighty. I have to write this letter in bits as each sentence drains me. I have not been out of shell range since March other than a week in July and even now I still find it strange not hearing the continual pounding. Oh it's just cleared enough and I have seen the white cliffs of Dover. Having wanted to I am now not sure I did, as I feel extremely sad.

18th August

British advance from Pozieres to Somme.

C Carver

Dearest Mum,

Things are a trifle dull here with still no end in sight. I suppose we shall struggle along trusting to luck and hoping we shall win through some how. Excuse such a mouldy line but news is scarce.

Much love from,

Christian

Dear Brother,

I don't think it would be wise to be in a hurry to leave school to join up. You will be of more use to the country if you can finish school. I know you want to be out here with me and if I could form a magic ring around you that protected you from shells, bullets, bayonets, Bosche and death it would be the one thing I would pray for most.

But the chances of us even meeting would be about a million to one. Besides, one of us being out here is enough and I hope that you will never have to see what I have seen. I sometimes think that all war is criminal folly and that the excuse that we were forced into it is no excuse at all. I have just got over a bad 4 days of flu and a slight reaction to the Somme I think.

I feel mentally run down and incapable of winding myself up again for the next push. The state of mind when you sit down and hate everything, shells, trenches, and the hopeless unending vista of more trenches and shells in the future can be hard to keep going. But it passes off I am glad to say.

Well tweet-tweet old bird, I am getting peckish,

Chick

19th August

Heavy fighting on Somme Front.

20th August

Artillery activity in Somme.

22nd August

Heavy aerial fighting on Somme Front.

C Carver

Dearest Mum,

Thanks so much for your letters and the cider and everything. We seem to have been forging on steadily on the Somme and we have nearly got the Bosche blindfolded for the winter. Things are fairly quiet and we are having good weather. Well tonnes of love to all,

Crick

28th August

Artillery activity on Somme Front. Germany declares war on Romania. Italy declares war on Germany.

C Carver

My dearest Mum,

Behold here we are back on the line again. Just in time as I was nearly bored extinct with boredom. Do you remember Kipling saying that the English don't mind being killed but the idea of being bored simply knocks them? And very true it is. We are off again tomorrow and our destination is as yet unknown but it will doubtless be a cauldron. As you may have gathered I have completely recovered from my fit of despondency. What I do say is, to quote my gunner's letter, 'roll on the end'. Much love from,

Christian

1st September

Bulgaria declares war on Romania.

C Carver

Dearest Mum,

I never got the chance of posting the last letter so by the time you get this it will have been a long time since you heard from me. Sorry. Great news about Bulgaria and Romania is it not? The jolly old German must be getting chilly to the feet, unlike myself, now that I have the excellent socks you sent me. I will have to mind my P's and Q's in future as I have been having quite a bit cut out by the censor. So has Carroll. No news or at least none I can tell you about. We go up to the line again tomorrow. One is never bored with this kind of fighting.

Tonnes of love to all,

Christian

8th September

C Carver

Dearest Mum,

Just a bit of a scrawl to thank you for all the letters. Weather here is fairly kind to us but the place looks such a mess. What a waste of shells. Great things go on all around us.

All my love,

Christian

H M Wilson

My dear Mother,

I am sorry my last letter was so brief. There is really no news I can tell you of. We have been having tea parties in Alex and the weather has been very hot indeed. I hope you got my letter saying I was now on the Mallow. I met up with Leslie and we talked about the Carver family till late.

Your loving son,

Hubert

13th September

C Carver

Dearest Mum,

Everything here is much the same as usual. I can't see how this war is going to end and its end is certainly not in sight yet. I suppose Germany is just going to run out of men though she could shorten her fronts considerably if she wanted.

This morning I played a very minor part in a push. A movie man was right beside me so you will doubtless one day see the battle. I was tempted to walk in front of him. Not long after he had finished filming we were shelled and buried to the waist. We have been seeing quite a few German prisoners lately and some of them can't be any older than 16!

Much love to all,

Crick

18th September

C Carver

Dearest Mum,

All goes pretty well here. The schools hols must be over now so wish them all lots of luck. Could you send me out another cardigan as my old one has recently joined the faithful departed. The fine weather we are having is still a little chilly. We have just had some really bad days when it has been real war and not playing soldiers. Everything is very uncertain and so I can't give any idea as to our future movements. The responsibilities of a Battery weigh more heavily in the rain. Heaps of things to be done so I must go.

Heaps of love to all from,

Crick

25th September

C Carver

Dear Dad,

Thanks so much for your letter. The weather here has been absolutely perfect and ideal for the push. We have no idea what our future holds but in the meantime just keep on fighting. During the last two months we have had a lot to do with the Australians and Canadians. As for the Canadians... well I am very glad I am not a Hun. They are simply grand. Well I suppose the house is empty of all us siblings. If I can get some leave we must all try to get together.

Heaps of love to all,

Crick

29th September

C Carver

Dearest Mum,

Thank you so much for the cardigan. It was just what was needed. We were brought up here in the morning of the 23rd and in the afternoon were ordered to bring the guns up too. Food was unable to reach us, which if you've eaten breakfast at 6 in the morning and nothing since having completed a strenuous day is not good news. All positions look the same. Like the jaws of hell. We got the food sorted by midnight. With September nearly over we have had some stirring times and some rough ones and have made some history in the last month too. We all grumble from time to time but wouldn't miss it for the world if the truth be told. Here England wins out against the heaviest odds the world has ever seen. What Ho she bumps! Heaps of love from,

Crick

2nd October

C Carver

My dear Dad,

Many thanks for the boots. We have just been looking at some letters captured from the German trenches. By Jove they do hate us. They seem to think that people like me were driven to war by the love of God. I find this offensive. There is a cage full of prisoners next to us with very interesting specimens. I hope the Zepps don't get too close to Birmingham,

love to all from,

Christian

⟜ 5th October ⟝

C Carver

Dearest Mum,

We are having a rotten old time. Not only are there lots of flies but now also newts and frogs a plenty. Pharaoh only had to put up with one plague at a time. He should try living here.

I suppose it doesn't help being so close to a river though that is best not spread. I have lost a lot of friends again just recently. I suppose it's all in a day's work. It's what it is beginning to feel like, love to all,

Christian

Dear Brother,

I did write to you a couple of days ago but when I re read it, it was such utter rot that I tore it up. The weather here is terrible which makes chances of another push less likely.

The two combined make me very cross. We have a nice mess at the moment thanks chiefly to loot from the last push. Please remember me to all,

Crick

⟜ 10th October ⟝

C Carver

Dearest Mum,

I had to travel well behind the Front to have my wisdom teeth out. I think that the experience was a milestone in my career due to the sheer pain. As I returned to the Front I could not even be cheered by passing German prisoners of war. Not even a smart salute from one of the German prisoners could stir me.

When we reached the Front we were told we were to move again. The wandering Jew is an absolute stay at home compared to us. I hope we get out to have a rest soon as the men need it. I wish you could meet Carroll, as he really is the salt of the earth and a very close friend.

Lots of love,

Crick

12th October

H M Wilson

My dear Mother,

It was very kind of Williams to send you a photo. I would like to see it very much. Nothing at all exciting has been happening lately. I don't suppose it will be long before we get the U-boats in the Atlantic under control.

Your loving son,

Hubert

17th October

C Carver

Dearest Mother,

Your guess as to where we are is perfectly correct. The Germans are getting a very bad time of it at the moment. I wish you could visit my observing station and I could show you the whole thing at a glance. In fact should Haig be knocked out you need not be anxious for right here is a worthy understudy! War has changed so much even while I have been at the Front. The idea of a 'push' is so different to what people really think it is. The Germans may be losing men but there are always more to take their place. The Germans are far better than we at picking ground to dig in though he did have a better selection all the way back in 1914. As we now take this better ground he is now feeling what we have felt. So much of our shelling has been fruitless due to his well-hidden artillery. Well that is no more.

Love to all,

Crick

23rd October

C Carver

Dearest Mum,

The teeth on one side are all but recovered but the wisdom teeth on the other have just started so I have another gruelling trip to the dentist soon. How we long to have the end in sight and to know that we have seen the worst time but it doesn't seem so at present but then it may all be nearer than we think. Francis has been asking about tanks.

Tell him yes, I have seen tanks aplenty. The mud has got very bad again but the tent I am in is like an oasis in the sea of mud. I am out of writing paper so could you send me some?

Much love from

Crick

29th October

C Carver

Dearest Mum,

Our principle topic of conversation here is, 'after the war,' and 'what will become of the other countries and us?' I have a very differing opinion with X who is so brave and has a brilliant mind but is devoid of feeling for the men and doesn't regard them for what they are worth. He doesn't feel the war will have changed anything.

I however feel, having lived in England and taken so much from her that I will never be able to repay all she has given me. I think life after the war will be as different as it is at the moment when compared to life before. We are no longer a nation with an army, the army is the nation and the nation its own army. Having been so unprepared and having been wrenched out of the comfortable groove by war – is it going to slip back into the old times of not begin ready? I can't believe that she will.

I know that once this is all over I shall not be choosing the army path for my future. I wouldn't mind doing two months a year to keep up to date though. I hate war but it is inevitable. Someone goes under, that is the meaning of war, but I don't see why it should be us. If we had had conscription at the start and could have faced Germany with a larger fully trained army would Germany have been so eager to look for trouble?

We must have looked a walk over. After this is all over I can see few that will relish conscription. War by all accounts should be for savages when one sees the sights I have seen. And yet it's the thinking men who can end this for us. It should not be called conscripting, it should be called patriotism.

Heaps of love to all,

Christian

4th November

C Carver

Dearest Mum,

I hate my label! It is red and on it is inscribed 2nd Lt. C C. Carver, RFA, C of E (from Birmingham) so would you get me a nice little identity disc and on it let there be engraved '2nd Lt. C .C. Carver, C of E' and on the other side put 'This Side Up' or 'Handle With Care' or something along those lines.

How silly he is! Let there be a chain to encircle his neck. We continue to wallow here in mud. Not a lot goes on here.

Heaps of love from,

Crick

6th November

C Carver

Dearest Dad,

This weather is very depressing as it is preventing us from continuing with our part of the push. I have just been censoring Sunday's crop of letters and am feeling very stupid indeed. We are growing rather stale with this weather so I am hoping we will be sent back for a rest and then some leave as the men do need it. I know though that I would feel lost without the noise as strange as that may sound.

We saw a terrific fire the other night. It was a French munitions dump and a very memorable site. I had a ride in a tank yesterday which was enthralling. No more really to say about this end.

Heaps of love from,

Crick

11th November

Canon Andrews

Oswin and I took part in the battle on the Serre and we had colossal casualties and as usual not much to show for it. We arrived at the dressing station filled with walking wounded and stretcher cases. All the doctors were very busy trying to do all they could for the badly wounded before they were taken away by ambulance.

The place was packed with suffering soldiers – smoking, shouting, only a few groans and some laughter. Oswin arrived and summed up the situation as only he could. The chaplains where standing about or doing what they could to help which was very little. Suddenly he boomed fourth, the doctors looked up from their patients for a moment and listened.

'What are all you chaplains doing here? You are useless; you are only getting in the doctors' way as they do their tremendous job. Far better for us all to go into the front line and help bring in some of the wounded. Parsons are like manure, they are all right scattered all over the country but when collected together they become a public nuisance. Come on Andrews, lets go,' and off we went to the front line.

Notes from Canon's Folly.

13th November

Fourth phase of Battle of the Somme begins.

C Carver

Dearest Mum,

The weather has at last consented to be kind while we administer an upper cut. I was very tired last night having had no sleep for the last 2 nights. I tend to be called out about 14 times a night. The show came off early yesterday morning.

The Battalion I was working with did splendidly. It seemed to be a bloodless defeat for the Bosche. At least I didn't see any dead. Almost unprecedented I should think.

It is an amazing feeling to walk forward over the ground we have been looking at and shooting at for the last month and a half. They have some splendid dugouts in which I am now settled. It is like an underground town about 30 feet under with nice bedrooms for the officers and bunks for the men. It had the look of a hasty abandonment with food still cooking and a half-empty glass of wine.

The Colonel being thirsty finished the wine off, only to discover it was neat whiskey out of the wrong bottle! I didn't know the Huns drank it. The lunch we had was fantastic, smoking Bosche cigars and drinking champagne. My bedroom is the neatest with the previous occupant's gas masks and bayonet all hung up and his book opened where he left off.

The only fly in the ointment was a message to say that if we wanted, the Brigade HQ would send up a prisoner who knew the location of the mine under the dugout! 'At once please,' was the answer. I hope leave shall be opened shortly and then I might get home for Xmas.

Much love,

Christian

21st November

C Carver

My dearest Mum,

A million pardons for nor having written for so long but we have been rather busy. The chilly weather and wind change has indeed brought snow. It came in under the eaves of my hut last night so that self and snipers were buried under a drift. I have realised I can't find it in me to dislike the individual German and dislike killing him intensely. Nothing further to report,

bags of love from,

Crick

22nd November

C Carver

Dear Dad,

Boredom is our portion. Nearly 22 weeks on the Somme is pretty nearly a record. And quite long enough. The weather delayed the last two attacks so leave has been put back too. The putting off of everything has made us utterly fed up. And a really good growl like this is the only relief. Dante would describe this area as torture in Hades. Men walking around in mazes, one foot in mud with shells bursting here and there and when a corner is turned there may be a body to remove and all the while being told that tomorrow rest is on its way. I have just censored another 50 letters. It is such a shame as so many of my men are such good writers. I smoke nothing but rank French cigars at present! When I get out I shall have a perfect orgy of good cigars. I grow more and more certain that the army is no place for me after the war. A railway runs close enough for me to hear as I go to sleep and I try to pick out that noise above the shelling. As a consequence I always dream I am in a train from Bristol going home. I must be gone,

love from,

Christian

C Carver

My dear Brother,

Life continues here with a push about once a week. I am looking after our horses at the moment and living in a tin hut which is more comfortable than it looks. There is much mud here. So glad school is going well. Keep it up!

Love,

Crick

25th November

C Carver

My dearest Mother,

It rains, steadily, monotonously, hopelessly, cruelly, exasperatingly it rains. We are expecting a change at the end of the month. What our fate will be heaven knows. The officers are being split up for a new scheme of redistribution. There may be a chance of leave when we get out of here. I can't wait. Comfy bed and endless baths.

Heaps of love from,

Crick

26th November

C Carver

My dear Dad,

The weather has been unspeakable these last two days and on top of that we are told we are to split up. One just has to smile and look as though one enjoyed it. Tact is the only way. I am not sure I am really supposed to be in this hut of mine. In a way I just pinched the place. Thus if someone bursts in having been told to come here they are rather surprised to see me. And they assume I am a Canadian and have a right to be here. I put on a nasal twang and say 'sure thing' and that usually sorts it but at some point I will have to leave it. I came close to it this morning. The Huns had been shelling around and about all night and it wasn't till they stopped that I really got to sleep. At 7.30 I was aware that the door was open and someone was trying to wake me up. He said I had to vacate within the hour as he was bringing men in and needed it. Not even when I told him my name was Haig and that I was the nephew of Sir Douglas did he relent. It all looked doomed so I packed up. But this evening I am still in possession and a little wooden cross marks the last resting-place of the would-be occupant! Well off to bed now.

Good night and heaps of love to all,

Crick

C Carver

Dearest Mum,

The land here is a wilderness of stinking liquid mud. So much for the earth, the air is fog. Great crows flap over the desolation croaking grimly. We were all ready to move out last night when the message arrived yet again that it had been cancelled. Ye little Gods of Mire and Strife who wouldn't be a soldier.

Heaps of love from,

Crick

PS what a life!

1st December

Lloyd George announces his departure from Government.

H M Wilson

Dear Mother,

Thank you for your letters. We are having quite a strenuous time now. We've had about three survivors from a torpedoed ship. The Euralyus is mine sweeping so we've heard. I am glad we don't do that any more. Some of the outbound mails have been sunk so you may be wondering if you are missing a few letters from me.

Your loving son,

Hubert

7th December

French regain trenches on Hill 304. Lloyd George becomes Prime Minister.

C Carver

Dearest Mother,

Finally we rest. There is nothing I enjoy more than a life of camp and caravan. Days on the road full of incident and humour and nights in villages. We are all muddy and tired. There are now vague hopes of leave.

Heaps of love,

Crick

14th December

C Carver

Ma Chere Mama,

We are immensely enjoying our rest and the exclusion of all cares and worries. Bath, shop, and be merry for tomorrow ... the mud. I think we can be pretty certain we shall return to the same place. Change is in the air and ones feels the beginning of a new chapter. The new government is thoroughly supported out here. England seems to be getting moving at last.

Germany too publishes to all the world that she too feels change but I hope it is for the worse. 1917 will be a black year for her. And what of the hungry souls in Germany and the weary desperate soldiers in France when the peace they have longed for and prayed for, the victorious peace they have been promised is refused? The weather is terribly unkind particularly for the horses. Their rest is standing in 2 feet of mud, as we have no stables for them. It breaks my heart.

Tonnes of love to all,

Christian

PS I have just fixed leave for Jan 8th for about 10 days so make sure the boys a get a little more holiday time as I would dearly love to see them.

26th December

H M Wilson

Dear Uncle,

The captain has asked me on behalf of himself and the whole of the ship's company to thank you for the turkeys you gave us. The men were most awfully glad to get them, as there was no fresh food in the ship on Christmas Day. We have been having bad weather just recently. This was my third Christmas at sea. The 'powers that be' are rather worried about the submarine business, which is rather serious. With all good wishes for the New Year.

Your affectionate nephew,

Hubert Wilson

29th December

Issue of Sir Douglas Haig's despatch dealing with Somme Battle. Murder of Russian monk Rasputin.

1917

1st January

Sir Douglas Haig promoted to Field Marshall.

C Carver

My dear Dad,

A very happy New Year to you all. You can expect me late on the 5th, all things being equal. I don't suppose this will reach you in time so I will try and wire later. Does it ever stop raining in this part of the world? We sometimes wonder with a dull apathy whether it rains like this in peacetime or is it merely woeful spite on the part of the weather.

Heaps of love,

Crick

4th January

C Carver

Journal entry by his mother

Christian arrived home on leave. We were having tea and the letters were just being sorted out so we didn't hear his taxi. He took us all by surprise arriving by the side door. A great shout from the boys and he came in. We all sat down to tea so joyful at having him with us at last. He produced presents for us all. He talked about the last six months when we were on our own and it was clear the last six months had been trying.

The outlook was grey and unending. He felt it was a reaction to the Somme. Hopes had been high before the Somme but November and December had come and gone with little change in positions. His father and brothers saw him off on Saturday. He had hoped they could all go to London together but trains and hotel accommodation were scarce. He took the disappointment so well. As it turned out, a good friend of his was in London to see him off.

14th January

C Carver

Dearest Mum,

Just a line to let you know that all is well so far. I am here in London and the ship sails at 11.30 and we are hoping for a smooth crossing. I shall probably go to Aberville and from there straight up to the front line at 4.20 tomorrow morning. It has been a topping good bit of leave and I only wish it could have lasted longer.

Love to all,

Christian

19th January

Canon Andrews

I had been asked to attend all condemned men since the first time and I had continued to do so – a harrowing experience every time. I had volunteered to do this on the understanding that I should act, if the men so wanted, as the prisoner's friend and defend him.

The barrister who not only was a friend, but also against shooting deserters, promised to help me in this matter. From that time on I was able to save all the men I defended from the death sentence.

As the war continued with ever increasing casualties my views on desertion had been slightly modified when it suddenly dawned on me what a tragic calamity and disaster can be inflicted upon hard pressed men holding the line if one of their number deserts.

There was one man I defended who had deserted five times and each time he was let off. I was to defend him and again with much persuasion saved him too. He assured me he would never desert again and on the next bombing raid he would be ready to go over the top. The Divisional Commander was furious with me for having got him off, saying he was sure to desert again and was a disgrace to the Division. I assured him I had straightened the man out. The following day I received a note to inform me my prisoner had again deserted under heavy fire. There was no trace of him anywhere. I decided not to go near the Divisional Commander for a bit. As it turned out I need not have worried. I was wounded that same night and had to be operated on and then sent back to London.

Notes taken from *Canon's Folly*, page 80.

C Carver

My dear Dad,

Behold me back in the abomination of desolation. I rode up here yesterday in a snowstorm. Things are still pretty rough up here and my dugout has 6 inches or so of mud and water on the floor. It's pretty chilly but one soon gets used to it. I had such a glorious leave the memory of which will carry me through many a long day. One always hears people coming back from leave say, 'Is it all worth it?' I can never understand that attitude. A well-trained memory like mine should be the sundial of life and only tell the sunlit hours. I wonder when my next will come.

Heaps of love from,

Crick

22nd January

C Carver

Hail brother,

It has been pretty mouldy getting back to war again. I had three nights in France en route and one at the wagon line. I got back to the Front in the middle of a snowstorm and it came upon me that this is a terrible war, a very terrible war. However I am now feeling a little brighter and more up for biffing or being biffed by the Bosche. We aren't doing much digging at present with the frost so things are fairly quiet. I don't think I have ever enjoyed anything so much as the leave I have just had. It really was top hole

Yours,

Christian

27th January

C Carver

My dear Dad,

I have dined and the stove is at last emitting sufficient heat to keep body and soul together. I am smoking some cigars and am probably more content than some 75% of the British Isles population. Isn't that an amazing thought?

The glare from the snow has been giving me some trouble particularly when there has been observing to do. But there is one great advantage to this cold weather. At least it is dry. This destroyer scrap seems to have been a nasty little cut at the Hun or so one hopes.

It is the most amazing piece of country. Simply no trenches because if either side dig a trench the other side promptly flatten it out with artillery. We just seem to float about in the open and the Hun does too. We have seen three Hun planes brought down in the last 2 days.

One of them was a most thrilling sight. In another the 2 men were captured unhurt. On being captured they said they thought they were landing in German trenches. Didn't want to admit it was our planes that forced them down. Surprising then that they fired the plane as soon as it landed with all the maps and drawings in it. On being taken the pilot said. 'These were not German trenches, no?' which was greeted by a chorus of, 'they were once, old man. They were once!'

It is a strange feeling to be walking freely over country that only last September one was having such narrow shave.

Please give my very best love to all,

Crick

31st January

Germany announces traffic of British Hospital ships between Great Britain, France and Belgium will no longer be tolerated.

1st February

British attacked near Wytschaete, with heavy casualties. Temporary suspension of all neutral sailing, in response to Germany's statement.

2nd February

C Carver

My dear Dad,

The cold here is perfectly frightful – you sit over a stove till one or more limbs are frost bitten and then rise and try and restore circulation. We have a few tame Bosche working for us in the horse lines. Thanks for all the letters and so glad the three boys are doing so well.

Love from,

Christian

8th February

C Carver

Very dearest Mum,

The cold is still very much with us. I have just spent the last 5 days in the wagon line where I have enjoyed a bath, hair cut and some wonderful lunches. As you may imagine our principle topic at present is the USA. We have moved into a new position while I have been away.

There is a difference between a place and a pig sty but it is nothing to the view one takes of a position on the day one leaves it compared to the day you occupied it. We look rather as if we had been washed up by the tide, as the ground has been so hard we haven't been able to dig ourselves in. It is beginning to loosen up a bit and so we are beginning to get somewhere.

I nearly killed the Major yesterday. Having lugged a sheet of corrugated iron up the steps of a former German shaft I dropped it and the Major was standing at the bottom. I am glad to say he is progressing favourably!

Love from,

Christian

17th February

C Carver

My dear brother,

One of the more offensive signs of spring is the large quantity of ammunition one is required to handle. For our doings today see the 'British Official'. Quite a goodly scrap. I nearly had my eardrums broken. Captured a good lot of prisoners who seemed very fed up with the whole thing.

The frost has been replaced by snow and so once again our universe turns slowly to mud. There is a smell of steam in the air as everything begins to warm up. With the thaw comes the appearance of boots – not so much objection to them but to their occupants.

The country is full of holes. The Somme is one immense battle field and tortured earth is scattered everywhere with debris, scores of shells, burst and otherwise, barbed wire, rifles, bombs and tonnes of kit of all sorts. There are no birds, only rats. We have moved forward again.

Heaps of love to all,

Crick

19th February

Action at Ypres. British inflict great damage on enemy positions.

C Carver

Dear Dad,

As you will have gathered from the papers we have been busy again hence my poor correspondence. Some day this story will be published and will stand as one of the most extraordinary pieces of heroism the British infantry have ever shown. A young 60 pounder stands not that far behind us here and blows out the candles every time he fires. One can't stand anywhere too long for fear of being engulfed by the mud. We had a fire next door to us yesterday. As you know water is brought up to us in petrol cans and they do sometimes get mixed up. Trying to set light to water is a fairly harmless exercise but when trying to boil petrol to make tea, well what can you expect? This mud makes you feel that running would be an impossibility. Enter a 'crump' and your theory was incorrect! One of my subalterns met a German prisoner a few days ago whom he had known well in America. What a small world. One of our battery commanders was very badly wounded today, reconnoitring the place we are moving into. A rotten job for he leaves (and I fear he must) a wife and two kiddies.

All my love,

Crick

2nd March

C Carver

My dearest Mum,

Just a quick scribble before we set off on our wanderings after the Hun. The weather is getting kinder to us. We seem to have been out of communication for some time. It is snowing heavily but we are comforting ourselves that March comes in like a lion and out like a lamb. I hope the boys are all ok

Love to all,

Crick

6th March

British line extended south of the Somme, twice the length of the year before.

13th March

Canon Andrews

Just before I was to return to the Front, having recovered, Oswin came over to London on leave. We had a wonderful few days enjoying all London had to offer. He got us all tickets for an opera. The box he had hired was crammed with his friends. In order for them all to have a seat he sat on the floor. There were two children sitting either side of him.

He was more concerned that everyone was enjoying themselves than what the actors were up to. The party afterwards was unforgettable. After this there were no more parties. No more family gatherings. It was his last leave. He never came back.

Notes taken from Canon's Folly, *page 90.*

C Carver

My very dearest Mum,

Here we are treading on the Bosche tail and not very gently either. We are pushing ahead almost too fast but at least we will soon be past this bit of country over which the worst fighting has passed. Perhaps you imagine it as a place of broken trees and ruined houses. In fact there is nothing. We live in this desolate belt from the Ancre to the Somme some five miles deep where no trees remain to make a show of green in the coming spring. The houses and churches are pounded to mounds of red and white dust. We have been living a rather nocturnal life recently due to the fact the Hun occupies the higher ground. The weary yellow moon guides us and looks as jaded as we are.

Much love,

Christian

16th March

Big advance on the Somme.

21st March

C Carver

My dearest Mum,

What a relief to get into decent country again. Quite a fitting finale to our long months of fighting in this part of the world for I believe we are for pastures new very shortly. The Russian news seems to be a bit of a bombshell but it all seems to be for the best. The French have done magnificently and one feels glad it fell to them to get civilians back again. We are in a range of fire which does not exude noxious fumes into the atmosphere and we can even get into pyjamas at night, an experience we have not enjoyed for the last 12 weeks.

We have to be so thankful to the Power that surely is, that we are the same company who came up in January. May the land we have just freed never have to feel the deathly hand of war again. We will be off soon to rest in the village where our wagon line was based in January.

The last bit of the push was really great fighting, regular open warfare again. We have come out of it all unscathed while people immediately in front and behind have paid a heavy toll. I am so glad we were here to see the final push having been part of it since July.

Love from,

Christian

22nd March

Heavy snow storms and increased enemy resistance.

2nd April

British advance continues.

C Carver

My dear Dad,

We are now in a quite different part of the world after quite a successful march. Picture if you may the scene we saw. A limitless expanse of water and mud, a team of horses are floundering along with a gun wallowing in their wake. I am likewise floundering along keeping up a stream of abuse and exhortation at the top of my voice.

The gun lurches drunkenly into a more than usually deep hole and stops with an air of finality. The gun does not shift an inch. I dismally contemplate following it into its grave and put an end to our troubles. We are not far from where we were last August and this time very comfortable.

Tons of love from,

Christian

5th April

C Carver

My dear brother,

How fearfully riling about your medical at Coventry. Of course it is only a question of trying other places till you find one to pass you or getting fitted with glasses? You can always get round things like that for such is our noble army. I feel sure it is simply the result of beaucoup de swot in an insufficient light. Keep on at them. We are having a very enjoyable rest at present; in fact we haven't had such a good time since we came to this fair land, what ho! The area is thick with farms that will to do all they can for you.

TOL,

CCC

6th April

USA declares war on Germany.

C Carver

My dearest Mother,

Easter Day. A most divine day, spring, belated spring at last. We have just been playing a little rough and ready cricket on a nightmare of a pitch.

Heaps of love from,

Crick

11th April

C Carver

My dear Dad,

Great rejoicing here over the push at Arras. For the last two months whenever things were not going well it has been all right, 'The push at Arras starts tomorrow'. We have not been out of the show since July and we feel quite lost. We had thought spring was coming in a rush but are now bogged down with blizzards. We are as pleased as you are about the Americans coming in. America joins, Germany makes an unsuccessful attack near Rheims and we get a good push at Arras. Bon! I am to be inoculated again, did I tell you?

Heaps of love to all,

Christian

12th April

C Carver

My dear old soul,

So bucked to hear you got through the teeth business by the skin of your eyes (that is vice versa). I have great hopes of getting three days with Mum in Rouen. It is raining here but then of course it would be. A splendid effort on Mum's part, surely she is the best ever.

The Hun is going under quickly we hope, at any rate he is getting every encouragement to do so. I have to thank Major Budden for arranging my three days leave. There are great happenings all along the Front. One has a feeling that anything might happen. This double line of trenches seemed so inflexible, so permanent that its break up gives a very positive sensation.

Love,

Christian

16th April

Second phase of Battle of the Aisne.

C Carver

Dearest Mum,

My leave has been confirmed for next week so I hope that will fit in with you. I do hope you have a smooth crossing as it begins to be such a long journey. We are at rest here but preparing to move in the next few days. Can't write much more now

Heaps and Heaps of love,

Crick

24th April

C Carver

Dearest Mum,

Come and have lunch with me at 1.15 at the Hotel de France. Just arrived, nine hours late, very dirty so need a little time before lunch with you.

Thine,

CCC

Mrs Carver

I went across to Rouen during the Easter Holidays to see a family friend who was dangerously ill from wounds and to try to meet up with Christian. He joined me on the 24th. While I waited I tended a grave of a man whose mother had been over to visit it, and I promised that while I was there I would tend it for her.

I had just sat down to lunch after this when I was given a note to say he (Christian) had arrived and was having a clean up. I sat and waited and soon he appeared, towel over arm, tousled hair and smiling. We felt it was so wonderful to have been given the chance of this meeting. He seemed so full of life and vigour. I felt full of life too when I realised how pleased he was that I had made the trip.

He spoke of his admiration for Major Bowen. We wandered all around. We knelt in some of the chapels. I spent much of the time expecting to be shot around every corner. He asked many questions about the family.

He expressed a very deep love and admiration for his father and I began to see how he had reached manhood. I became very struck by some of the French officers we had seen in the chapels. Motionless in prayer with their great blue coats wrapped about them. I longed for the train to take him back to the Front to be delayed as sometimes happened, and it did get delayed till Saturday, so we did get one day extra. I know Christian was desperate to get back, as he knew they were short of hands since his departure. I wanted him to take plenty of fresh fruit with him, which I knew he loved but he would only consent to me buying him dates. He became quite cross over me pushing him to buy apples.

As much as he wanted to return to the Front, he desperately wanted to return home with me. We arrived at the station and Christian peered in at the windows of the train to see if there were any free seats. He eventually found one and marked it with his coat and luggage and returned to the platform with me. He walked a little way to one of the bridges and we said our farewells. It had been such an ideal time and we had so enjoyed it. The weather had been lovely and as usual Christian was in his wonderful loving unselfish way. I returned to the hotel to pack as I was returning to England the next day.

26th April

H M Wilson
HMS Mallow

My dear Mother,

We got in yesterday, the second anniversary of the landing and it was wonderful to receive all your letters. I am hoping for a change of job soon as I am feeling rather fed up. Williams, who is my greatest friend out here, is going home for a bit from the Magnolia. His brother who has a lot to do with the big people at the admiralty managed to get it worked.

Practically all my friends have gone home which makes it even worse. Two and a half years out here without leave is quite long enough I feel. I wonder whether father being in town so often could sort something. Things continue much the same out here. Please don't trouble yourself over this but if you do happen to see Carson in town would you do something about it.

Your affectionate son,

Hubert

30th April

C Carver

My dearest Mum,

Behold me at the War again. As I travelled up to the line I heard that the division had still not moved and then I heard that they had and that they were on the march so no one knew where they were. I made the decision to push on and try and find them. After many lifts in lorries here and there I found them and we are to be going into action tonight. At least this way I avoid an anticlimax by arriving straight back in as it were.

I had such a lovely time but I am not sorry to be back at the elemental life again. One cannot do without it after a time. It must be like drink or something! I do hope you had a safe journey back. I don't know what I should have done without the basket of provision you insisted I take. The remains of the chicken are still acting as a strategic reserve.

Any amount of love to the family from,

Crick

Stephen Williams

After the April 1917 losses, regulations appeared to sufficiently relax to enable a return in time to partake in the brilliantly organised success of Messines. Plumer's achievement was probably the only large operation which has ever approached its anticipated timetable.

During the subsequent lull our air support was so conserved for forthcoming events that the Bosche was unmolested in the sky; we even lacked any anti-aircraft guns in the fighting area. One day we saw the unique spectacle of a plane going down the line of our captive observation balloons and bursting all eleven of them. They came down in flames, with the dual observers all coming down in their white parachutes amidst their pall of black smoke.

A German air formation of high repute was Ricthoven's, well known by sight by their scarlet bodies and white wings, and daily these swaggered around our heads, finishing their visit by detaching on to dive with his machine gun blazing at our front line troops. As this became regular and we naturally knew the exact range to the line of trenches concerned, it was worth while trying to scare this menace off, so we laid up to have a dab at him with a field gun. Next day he arrived on his usual mission and our first shell missed him, bursting just behind his tail. In spite of the impracticability of traversing to compete with his speed, the gun was swung over with such judgement that the layer cracked the second round into his amid ships and so the plane fell among the objects of its destruction. They never repeated the nuisance after that, although it was frankly an almost incredible performance for 18-pounder equipment.

In this newly occupied ground we first saw the able German engineering construction of pillboxes, generally quite shell proof and of reinforced concrete. Their apparatus now faced the wrong way, but they provided safe cover during intermittent bombardments, although when struck by a heavy shell the concussion would snuff out candles, as well as giving the occupants the most stunning headaches.

⟜ 1st May ⊸

Stephen Williams

My own battery Commander was a cold and hard but very able master, probably perfect for a lad in need of polishing! He had seen much experience on the Indian Frontier and never outwardly showed any signs of either impulsiveness or fear. Not even during that long and most severe test of the Battle of the Somme. Yet, quite coolly, one morning early in June 1917, he said that he knew he was destined to be killed the following day. He took his premonition quite unmoved, except to try and extract promises from his superiors regarding his replacement.

Early next morning as he rode up Messines Hill, followed by a mounted observation party, a lone shrapnel shell burst over his head. It is certainly quite impossible to predict how any particular individual will behave in a fight, as this bears no relation to ordinary visible characteristics. Some of the stars of athletic contests are rotters when it comes to a real scrap. Some of the most mice-like creatures are liable to brilliantly excel, but there is no method of knowing beforehand with unproved material.

In my own case, the 1st phase of the fighting was proving an increasing strain of hiding fear, and curiously, the 2nd phase, in spite of its greater intensity, saw me become more and more indifferent. It is all very important as the slightest sign of fear or lack of confidence is extremely infectious, and is flashed through subordinates and with emphasis.

C Carver

My dear Dad,

I am writing this from New Zealand. Well nearly. The dug out I am in is the deepest I have ever seen. All is much the same as usual. I had a simply splendid holiday with Mum in Rouen.

The Hun gave us a famous welcome when I got back to the Front. But these are indeed dark times for him and I think most of them are asking how is it all going to end and as yet they dare not face the answer. I must retire now, as I have to be off at 3.30am tomorrow.

Love to all,

Crick

3rd May

W H Carver

The 10th attacked along half a mile of the Front in the Battle of Oppy Wood, north east of Arras. Losses were high.

Notes taken from The Trench.

5th May

C Carver

My dear brother,

Many thanks for your letters. Rouen was wonderful. I have a feeling that somehow it will have a great place in my life. The fighting is pretty stiff and I can't say too much about it of course but we are enjoying it on the whole. The weather has been really hot for the last week but we expect thunder later on today.

Yours,

CCC

6th May

C Carver

My dearest Mum,

It was such a delightful time we had together and I feel sure we shall never forget it. A sort of little oasis in the desert of war. I feel now more than ever that I do not deserve the love you lavish on me. Someone once wrote, 'A few men are born worthy of their mothers, but hardly any die worthy of them.' I often think how true that is.

The Germans are putting up a desperate fight all along the Front, desperate because behind them lies the chasm of defeat. We feel so fresh we are attacking with a new zest. While the Major is here we are a happy family. I imagine the boys will be back at school by the time this gets to you.

Love to Dad,

Christian

10th May

C Carver
A nasty dug-out

Dear Uncle,

I commence this letter bored to extinction. And the worst of it is that you would not appreciate the extreme bitterness of my lot were I to retail it. These German dugouts are on the same plain, 2 shafts about 25 yards apart leading down some 30 feet underground and connected at that depth by a corridor. Very safe. This particular one is inhabited by a cat who forgot to retreat with the Bosche when they did. It's recently become the mother of rather a large family. The question is, what nationality are they? Born of a German mother on French soil in an English Colonel's tin hat.

I was made to be a thinker rather than a doer. Everything went as it should have done till I was 18 and since then I have had a taste of danger and adventure and as much as I like it, life would be awfully dull with out it. We men are hurled into a cauldron of war and come out changed. I hope when I return to peace there are some little wars I can take part in.

When I arrived I disliked war, the ugliness, the dirt, the blood, and was horribly frightened of shells. Now I don't particularly mind shells and I enjoy the work and the danger and all this great game of chance and skill.

We will be out for a rest in the next few days in a village recently destroyed by the Hun. It is very sad to sea all the fruit trees cut down, poor things, they are flowering away bravely for the last time.

Yours,

C Carver

15th May

C Carver

My dearest Mum,

By Jove! War is almost worth it in this kind of weather and I am enjoying the scrapping in a kind of way. We have had a moderately hot time but our luck as usual has held. The wagon line plays cricket every night and so do we all now we are out for a weeks rest. The two balls you sent me last summer are seeing much use. I would be very grateful if you could send a few more and a bat would be useful as our second one is somewhat incomplete. My bowling is positively brilliant on a French wicket.

Heaps of love to all from,

Crick

18th May

C Carver

My dear Brother,

The country round here is rather an enigma – I think because the social life has been utterly wiped out from it. On the one hand you have the Front, which is always the same, a place of shells and dust and every kind of scrap, and on the other is France, the place of the French. But this is half way land. Not knocked about at all but every kind of human habitation, every bit of human handiwork has been destroyed. The people are carried off and such as still survive in Hun land will probably never come back to these ruins of evil memory. The land is not properly French or German and only superficially English. Too mentally paralysed to write any more fantastic rot.

Yours,

C Carver

20th May

End of second battle of Aisne.

C Carver

My dear Dad,

I am enjoying the battle on the whole but it is an acquired taste. Leave has just opened again so I am beginning to entertain hopes for getting home somewhere between the end of July and the beginning of August. We have just got back from the wagon line after a very peaceful time there.

We arrived back to a long day of battle, as your papers will probably tell you. Is it possible that in this our great hour Russia may back down? It seems unthinkable but I suppose it has to be faced. Some more reading material would be very welcome by the way. It is fearfully hot tonight so I will give up this trash.

Heaps of love to you,

Crick

26th May

C Carver

My dearest Mum,

We have just moved into a new fighting home. I had only just finished my last letter to you when we became the object of some hate. I have just put in the four most strenuous days of my lazy life digging solidly during the hours of daylight and I have now the satisfaction of seeing us pretty safely under France in dugouts to the design of CCC

Heaps of love from,

Christian

29th May

C Carver

My dearest Mum,

I am so awfully sorry to hear you have been ill. I do wish I was with you at home but perhaps with a love like ours it doesn't matter how far apart we are. Thanks so much for sending the cricket things. All continues well.

Nothing like a really hard winter to make one appreciate small mercies of a warm summer. Things are going fairly satisfactorily don't you think? The Italians are doing good work.

This is a very dull letter I fear but one mustn't write too much about the game, as interesting though it would be to you.

Much love from,

Christian

31st May

Artillery action at Ypres.

1st June

Continued artillery action duel in Wytschaete salient.

3rd June

C Carver

My very dearest Mum,

I am awfully bucked up to hear you are on the mend. Once you are up and about on your pins again please take life more slowly and try not to leave the house before 7am without having had breakfast. We would all feel happier if you did. I feel now more than ever that your prayers are a very real protection to us and that something is guarding us in a wonderful way.

Heaps of love,

Crick

7th June

Battle of Messines begins. British capture Wytschaete ridge after setting off 19 mines and storm nine miles of the Front.

10th June

British continue to gain ground along Messines region.

C Carver

My dear Dad,

I am so pleased to here Mum keeps on improving. I am enjoying a 4-day rest in the wagon line. The horses look fantastic and my blacks, especially my blacks. Great rejoicing here over the show up north. The Bosche High Command must be having some nasty moments. I think tank racing will be a great feature in times to come. What wonderful times we do live in! Wasn't it rough luck Pip being shot down – it is appalling how many fellows one knows who have gone out lately. During this last year I have been in the fire with the rest and have emerged as something different. The iron entering into the soul is a very real process for although the battle is the stiffest and hottest we have met yet, I enjoy the life and the deed and the danger and even in some queer way the very fear, as I have never done before.

Love to all,

Christian

22nd June

C Carver

My very dearest Mum,

We are not fighting at the moment and having a most enjoyable time sitting easy. 2 days before we came here a 5.9 pitched in a dugout containing one of my detachments, killing one and burying 4, 3 of which have had to leave due to shock. All very sickening. We are having a splendid time prior to going in for a perfectly different venture elsewhere. Having had two impossible chargers I am now in possession of two grand replacements which Sparke my groom is very relieved about as he is the one who has to ride them the most,

heaps of love to all,

Crick.

25th June

First contingent of American troops lands in France.

Stephen Williams

Dear Mother and Father,

Just a short line to let you know I am getting on A1. I should be very pleased if you could send out a snaffle bit for my horses as they have both got very good mouths and I only have the army curb thing. As for food we have plenty here so any sent would just go to waste. A longer letter next time, love to all from,

Stephen

PS I was back yesterday and had a hot bath!

29th June

C Carver

My very dearest Ma,

So glad to hear you are getting on steadily. There is a chance I may get some leave in 10 days or so. Will let you know more as soon as I do.

TOL,

Crick

3rd July

C Carver

My very dearest 'old dear',

We are still in the rest game and the plunge bath is now full of green weed and not without odour. We go to the Front tomorrow. I have been walking a lot in this country as I feel that our destination is going to be very different from the peace and beauty that surround us at the moment.

Heaps of love to you,

Crick

8th July

Stephen Williams

The dawn of my 21st birthday, 8th July, broke for me in a fighter's role. A role I may say I seem to have had to experience as much of as any Briton living of my own age, and far more than any I am acquainted with, although, paradoxically, no one can be more peace loving than I am. That dawn was spent in the shattering orgy of getting ammunition teams through Ypres City. From the Cloth Hall to the Menin Gate was a particularly bad bottleneck. Nearly the whole supply traffic of the Ypres Salient had to pass through this at night somehow. The Bosche knowing we were then mounting a big scale attack, kept up a steady rain of shell and gas shell on that area, causing havoc amongst the columns and, in turn, inescapable and disastrous road blockages. The Battery's initial position was in the eastern fence of Les Ecoles with a zone of fire centred on Hooge. Things were hard up then and, no doubt, we must all have shown the strain of it with hard unnatural appearances. It was amusing one morning, when having just spent all night on an intense bombardment, our Gunner Commander, a fine type of Brigadier arrived in this softness of appearance of staff and luxury from the rear areas. We were all well acquainted with one another but after welcoming him and showing him the layout he stared at me grimly and in a perplexed way said, 'Is one of your officers anywhere about?'

9th July

C Carver

My very dearest Mum,

I am afraid my leave is off. We are in a new place now and there doesn't seem to be much leave going. Sickening luck. Sorry for having got your hopes up. Thank you very much for the birthday letters. Tomorrow we go on to a place where we stayed last August. (Near Ypres). Well I hope my leave comes up again within the next month.

Heaps of love from,

Crick

Christian was now twenty.

11th July

C Carver

My dear Dad,

We have arrived at our final destination and back at the war in earnest. I don't mind for myself that leave was cancelled as after the next few months I will feel like I deserve it more. I wish I could tell you all our doings but of course all is a sealed book. These 2 years have been pretty full of adventure and the next few months bid fair to beat the lot. Well goodbye and bless you my dearest Dad, I am sure your prayers will help us in the days to come as they always have done.

Heaps of love,

Crick

13th July

C Carver

My dear old brother,

This is a letter that I always approach with reluctance. It's just before we sally forth into battle and suppose it should be the last – what a rotten one! Midnight is the appointed hour and the spot is no health resort. However I have always bobbed up smiling from these horrid places and I hope to continue to do so. I have just missed out on leave but at least after this next battle I will be the first to go. I wouldn't want to leave the battery just now anyway. This is a very critical time everywhere and we all have to stick by our jobs as best we can. Well cheer thee ho, old buck, and a merry journey along the road.

Yours,

C Carver

17th July

Successful British raids in Ypres sector.

19th July

C Carver

My dearest Mum,

We are taking part in an immense artillery battle the like of which has never been seen before. No one-sided affair this but two strong opponents going bald headed at each other. The story of our recent adventures must wait until I am home. Major Budden has been slightly wounded but is still with us and I have lost a couple of friends, which will be sad news for Caroll when he returns from leave. We are situated on the banks of a considerable lake, which must be lovely in peacetime. What do you make of the sign of the times? We have had two fairly exasperating gas nights with helmets on for three hours. At such times one can only sit and think and wait. It is then that I say to myself, 'Lighten our darkness we beseech Thee oh Lord and by Thy great mercy defend us from all the perils and dangers of this night, and give me tranquillity and self control and loyalty so that I may do that which Thou hast given me to do.' Letters are also a great blessing too. Of course we do have some happy times. There has to be if we are to attain to the great good that is coming to us through the glare of battle. This, to put it mildly is a most damnable bloodsome spot the wretched field batteries seem to get everything that is going and there is plenty. We shall be glad to get on and over. There is such a lot of infernal waiting and wondering if the next will have your number on it. These times of trial do at least bring out the best in people. You get down to the truth, which is the best kind of beauty. Reading this over it sounds a paltry morbid effort but I assure you I am not really morbid and I am very much in love with the gunner's life.

Tons of love from,

Crick

21st July

Heavy artillery battle in Flanders.

22nd July

C Carver to the mother of his groom, Sparke.

Dear Mrs Sparke,

I have just heard with the utmost dismay that your son has been wounded. I am hoping it is nothing serious and will let you know details when I get them. I don't know what I shall do without him, my cheery little Sparke, for there was never a better man with horses and I shall never have such a groom again. He happened to be hit on the same road as your other gallant son was killed on, perhaps almost the same spot. Perhaps this will be the first you have heard of it. In which case this will have come as rather a bombshell I am afraid. A horrid war when such things happen. I will send you a cheque for the money I owe him. Believe me no one could sympathise with you more and I remain yours sincerely,

C Carver

Charles Sparke, his groom appears to have died on the 17th, aged 20.

23rd July

Numerous raids by British and Canadians.

24th July

C Carver

The Carver family is informed that Christian had been wounded by a shell in the thigh and knee.

25th July

Intense artillery battle in progress in Flanders.

C Carver

No news came.

26th July

C Carver

A letter written on the 24th informed his family that Christian had died of wounds late the previous night. The same shell had hit him and his Major on the morning of the 23rd and he was severely wounded in the thigh, which was fractured, and slightly in the knee.

The doctor was on the spot and looked after him at once and sent him off so that he was in hospital within a few hours. Every attention had been given him but the shock killed him. The hospital wrote to say he had been very weak and had only lasted a few hours at the hospital. He had asked for his parents to be informed he was only slightly wounded. The Chaplain was with him when he died and commended his soul to God. It was a very peaceful ending and he suffered very little. The Major was still in a critical condition. Christian took it all very well and never murmured. His body was buried at the Lyssenhoek Cemetery.

27th July

Further fighting north of the Aisne.

31st July

3rd Battle of Ypres begins.

Stephen Williams

The infantry, after colossal preparation, moved forward in the most costly battle of Passchendaele, on the 31st of July. The subsequent appalling details are as well relegated to the care of history. No one there can ever obliterate all its tragedy from memory. Every inch of ground on both sides appeared to have been pulverised by shellfire although many troops survived. The rains brought a sea of mud worse than ever we had already experienced. A deep and holding mud which made it a hard struggle for a fit man to wend his way across but quite defeated and swallowed up the gassed or wounded. So death overtook an abnormal number.

1st August

C Carver

Dear Mrs Carver,

I am so very sorry for having been so long in writing again. I hope you will make allowances knowing that we have been hard at it in preparation for one of the most extensive battles the world has ever seen. I went down this morning to find out where Christian had been buried and to see his grave. Major Bowen is buried there too. These are the details I have heard so far. They had been standing together outside Christian's dugout. They heard a shell and jumped for the dugout but unfortunately the shell landed on top of it. Christian was hit in the thigh and Major Bowen had both his legs shattered.

From what I can hear they were hurried to the dressing station and then onto the clearing station at Poperinghe. I believe Christian's death was chiefly due to shock. Major Bowen died as a result of complications after both his legs had been amputated. Christian's belongings are being organised and will be dispatched to you shortly. Many who knew him have expressed their deepest sympathy. He had so many admirers who will miss him deeply.

Major Bowen so often used to say to me that he hoped your son would never be hit and it seems so strange that they should have been hit together. Christian told me after his leave had been cancelled before moving to Ypres that he was so very sad about it and he so wanted to see you all as he felt sure he would never see you again. I told him not to be silly, but perhaps he knew better. He again told me the last time I saw him on the 16th. I have just met a driver from Christian's Brigade who was on leave and he told me that few of the old lot were left, both men and horses. They tell me they had every hope for him once they had dug him out and put him in the ambulance. Had the Major survived he would have told you in what high regard he held your son and how beloved and efficient he was. Major Bowen died two days after Christian.

Yours very sincerely,

E Budden

8th August

Wet weather continues in Flanders.

10th August

British continue to advance east of Ypres.

22nd August

Heavy fighting on the Ypres Front. British advance 500 yards.

28th August

French positions at Verdun restored to what they were before February 1916 attack.

12th September

By end of July, German losses estimated at 4 million.

15th September

Second phase of Third Battle of Ypres. British continue advance east of Ypres.

9th October

Third phase of Third Battle of Ypres begins. One mile advance on Passchendaele Ridge.

Stephen Williams

In October the 25th Division went to Bethune and took over the Fuesthubert Line, immediately on the right of the Portuguese. These people were a useful lot of cut-throats but language prevented us becoming well acquainted with them.

30th October

British attack Passchendaele but later driven back to outskirts.

2nd November

Hostile artillery activity east of Ypres.

6th November

End of Third Battle of Ypres.

7th November

British consolidate new positions at Passchendaele.

1918

Stephen Williams

The Military Cross was awarded to Stephen Williams on 26th of May 1918 at Chalons Le Verguer. At this time he was a Lieutenant in the Royal Field Artillery (the same as Christian Carver). It was for conspicuous gallantry and devotion to duty when the approaches to the battery were being heavily shelled with gas and the road was blocked with dead horses and debris. He, though suffering from gas, rode through a heavy barrage and cleared the lower part of the road, thus enabling the battery to get into action. He was wounded twice, the second time near the end of the war, and had his right ear shot and was stone deaf in that ear for the rest of his life. Convenient, he always said, if he didn't want to hear, but the other ear missed nothing.

Canon Andrews

Early in 1918 I was posted back to my old division. I met the General again whom after asking after my wound told me firmly not to let any more deserters off. When I reached the Front they were preparing for a big German offensive.

Notes taken from Canon's Folly.

21st March

Germany launches spring push, eventually mounting five major offensives against Allied forces.

9th April

Germany launches second Spring offensive.

Canon Andrews

In April the great German offensive we had been waiting for broke through on a very misty morning with only a few yards visibility. We could see the Germans all around us. It felt like this could be the end but though badly bruised we managed to retire. We regrouped and that evening went back into battle with the reserves mostly being young boys. They fought like seasoned warriors in the fiercest shelling I have ever experienced.

When the battle was at its height I came across Oswin with his gunners. He was on his big horse getting the horses to run the guns up to the ridge where they could see the Germans breaking through. When there was a lull in the fighting he came over a talked with me for a while. When he was needed again he turned to leave and shouted over his shoulder 'when this hell is past we must go on leave together' and I watched him disappear slowly into the smoke. The following day I met a runner from the gunners who shouted to me across the road as he rushed along 'The Padre stopped a shell yesterday sir. Now 'ees gone, 'e was always asking for it. We shall never 'ave another like 'im.' Oswin after he had left me had volunteered to undertake the job of burying the men for the whole Front.

Going up to a battery position he was speaking to two of his gunners when a shell burst and killed all three of them. He was buried in the nearby cemetery with the two soldiers either side of him. I felt this was the end. I walked about dazed. I could still here his voice booming forth. I was rung later that evening by Bishop Gwynne, who invited me over. The real reason was to help us stop thinking about Oswin. Not long after this I was appointed Chaplain of an Australian squadron near the Front. I met up with some friends who I had not seen since Gallipoli.

Notes taken from Canon's Folly.

15th July

Final phase of great German spring push. Second Battle of Marne begins.

16th – 17th July

Former Tsar Nicholas II, wife and children murdered by Bolsheviks.

18th July

Allies counterattack German forces, seizing initiative.

8th August

Haig directs start of successful Amiens offensive, forcing all German troops back to the Hindenburg Line; Ludendorff calls it a 'black day' for German army.

27th September – 17th October

Haig's forces storm Hindenburg Line, breaking through at several points.

29th September

Bulgaria concludes armistice negotiations.

28th September – 14th October

Belgian troops attack at Ypres.

3rd – 4th October

Germany and Austria send peace notes to US President Woodrow Wilson requesting an armistice.

Canon Andrews

In the month of October we were marching on and this was one of the happiest and saddest times of the war for me. There they were, the pick of Australia's youth going into bat like their fathers before them, knowing that sooner or later they must be out, for few carried their bat for the entire innings. I felt so useless waving these brave men off, some of them never to return. We were advancing everywhere with colossal casualties and devastating destruction. We had tried so hard to believe that the suffering and sacrifice were the offering men and women make to end all wars. People's faith was damaged. They felt a good God would not have allowed this to happen. I felt my job was going to be made much harder when it was all over.

Notes taken from Canon's Folly, *page 97.*

17th October – 11th November

British advance to the Sambre and Schledt rivers.

21st October

Germany ceases unrestricted submarine warfare.

7th – 11th November

Germany negotiates an armistice with the Allies in Ferdinand Foch's railway carriage Headquarters at Compiegne.

9th November

Kaiser Wilhelm II abdicates.

10th November

Kaiser Wilhelm II flees to Holland. German Republic is founded.

11th November

Armistice Day; fighting ceases at 11 am.

Letter written by my Great Aunt Peg (daughter of W H Carver) to her cousin, Rosemary Maxsted.

Oh Darling,

Isn't it wonderful news – this morning at 10.22 I was in the room where the tape machine is (we are simply glued to it always). I saw news come through 'Armistice signed' – so of course we knew there would be great joy and that people would go at once to Buckingham Palace. So off we all went, Ma and Pa and Little Peg at 11 o'clock when hostilities ceased. Maroons were fired and the crowd were simply great but most awfully well behaved in front of the Palace; boys climbed all over the monument. The police tried to keep them down but of course no use, they sat on the heads of the figures and everywhere!! – Well the King (God bless him) came out with the Queen and the Duke of Connaught and Princess Mary in a V.A.D. uniform and the crowd cheered like mad and we all sang 'God Save The King'. Then they went in and the crowd got thicker and thicker. We had a very good place on the steps of the monument. You should have seen the taxis! Each one with at least 14 people on it, outside and inside and on the bonnet! Oh I did wish you had been with us. Well the crowd yelled and yelled 'WE WANT KING GEORGE' about every moment. All too thrilling for words.

I had seen the Duke of Connaught go off somewhere earlier on in the morning and now he came back right down the steps with Princess Pat (Pa got a doff from both of them). We were absolutely next to see Princess Patricia who simply grinned at him and the Duke returned his salute! Then they went into the Palace and the massed bands of the Guards came out and the King came out again. And we all sang 'Keep the Home Fires Burning', 'Tipperary', the Doxology and all the Allies' anthems and a few others, and at the end of each we cheered and yelled, 'We want a speech' and at last the King spoke.

I was very nearly at the Palace gates with Ma and I could just hear what he said, of course you know it, (probably know all this much better than I do, but I thought you would like to know 'eye witness' biz.!!! Oh if only you had been there with us). Well where had I got to. Oh yes the King made a short speech and we and most of the crowd went away, of course still yelling! I had asked Steve to come and spend the afternoon with me; her hours off are from 2 to 6. We came in from the Palace about 1.45 so she came up to us at lunch (food at the top of the house and coming down in the lift always makes me sick!!!) and after lunch we went and saw the 'Houses' go to a thanksgiving service at St Margaret's. Everyone was still on the cabs and everything and oh you know flags and a few absolutely tight. Ma came home and Pa, Steve and I went on down to Whitehall to the Horse Guards and through the Admiralty Arch to show Steve the Hun Guns in Pall Mall – simply heaps you know. Well it was all very thrilling and I wouldn't have missed it for anything and now I am writing with the blinds up and the light full on! We were going home tomorrow but now Pa says Wed. He might have let me come down to see you

Very best love,

Patricia.

Epilogue – After the War

January 10th – 15th

Communist revolt in Berlin.

January 18th

Start of peace negotiations in Paris.

January 25th

Peace conference accepts principle of a League of Nations.

May 7th – June 28th

Treaty of Versailles drafted and signed.

June 21st

German High Seas Fleet scuttled at Scapa Flow.

July 19th

Cenotaph unveiled in London.

Tudor St John

Of my wounds and how they progressed I don't intend to write much. Illness is mercifully easy to forget and is best forgotten but I cannot close a record of my war experiences without referring to those who have shown so much kindness to me during sickness and convalescence. To begin with I was badly hit, so badly so, indeed, that at the clearing hospital at Bailleul they did not think it worth while to move me from my stretcher to a bed which might be needed for someone with more chance of living through the night. All through too I was attended by extraordinary pieces of good luck. At the very commencement I was lying on my face when hit in the neck. Had I been lying on my back I must have died at once. Then I suppose I am the only man who has been shot in that region where I was hit and whose throat the bullet has gone through without touching any of the three or four vital parts which are there grouped.

While still recovering from his wounds in 1916, he volunteered to take over as editor of The St. George's Gazette (the Regimental magazine) and so continued to serve the Northumberland Fusiliers, which he could no longer join in the field. He remained in this post for 31 years and it was said at the time of his death that he had given 47 years of faithful service to his Regiment.

While at this post, a group of philanthropists, headed by Lord Wittenham also secured him a job as HM Deliverer of The Vote on the Speaker's Staff in the House of Commons. He was also provided with the Old Mill House on Wittenham's estate at Benson beside the Thames above Wallingford. When Lord Wittenham died his widow was compelled to sell the estate and so the family moved to Aboyne, Aberdeenshire. It was here that Major St. John died aged 84 in 1965.

Notes taken from A Tale of Two Rivers.

Alfred Williams comparing the differences of Army and Naval life during war.

Young boys in their 20's both officers and men, had terribly long hours. In fact I suppose that if they were in an active part of the line they must have been ready for action for as long as they were on duty and until they were relieved, with desperate fighting at any time. Also, I suppose, at times they had long intervals of inactivity, but often up to their knees in mud and in great discomfort.

On board ship we always had a bunk or sofa to rest on in the daytime and we slept in hammocks at night. Our hammocks were stowed in bays on the upper deck where coaling the ship took place. After about a month someone had the bright idea that our hammocks should be inspected (we slept in hammocks slung below decks with one sheet and blankets) and in daylight their colour was nearer that of coal than of canvas. As war conditions were easing up a bit by then there was a hell of a row and our hammocks were inspected weekly for sometime afterwards. The most strenuous twenty-four hours I can remember was keeping the morning watch.

Alfred Williams married his first wife Audrey Rogers in 1920. She died in July 1943. He then married my grandmother (W H Carver's younger daughter Dorothy Veronica Carver) whose first husband, Frank Robins, had been killed at El Alamain in the Second World War. Alfred Williams died in 1985 having, amongst other important jobs, served as a Member of Parliament for North Cornwall (1924–1929) and had for sometime been in charge of minesweeping operations in the Suez during WW2.

H M Wilson

Known as 'King', he married Patricia Carver, my grandmother's sister. He served again in the navy during the Second World War with the convoys from America. He died in 1977.

Stephen Williams

Died in 1958 having served in the Second World War.

W H Carver

Died in 1961.

Canon Andrews

A Queen's chaplain, he married my parents in 1974. Died in 1989, aged 102.

Bibliography

The Trench

Copyright Richard van Emden 2002 – by arrangement with BBC. Published by Bantam Press, (division of Transworld Publishers). All rights reserved.

Canon's Folly

Canon Andrews autobiography. Published in 1974 by Michael Joseph Ltd and printed by Tonbridge Printers Ltd.

A Tale of Two Rivers

Michael St John's autobiography. Published in 1989 by Bushmain Publishers, Aylesbury.

Website

www.greatwar.com

The National Archives, Public Records Office

Details of the sinking of HMS Russell

ADM1/8455/97 Loss of HMS Russell, Court Martial 1916

Privately Supplied Memoirs

Tudor St John – 1914 Diary.

Alfred Williams – Memoirs.

Stephen Williams – Notes written while World War II prisoner in Tobruke.

John Williams – Diary and letters.

Robert Williams – Letters.

W H Carver – Diary and letters.

Hubert Wilson – Letters.

Christian Carver – Trench letters (printed by his family with additions by his mother.)

Notes on sources

1914

p49	'The Kaiser and God' reprinted from A Treasury of War Poetry. Ed. George Herbert Clarke. Boston: Houghton Mifflin Co., 1917.
p51	'At around 7.30pm...' Richard van Emden, The Trench, p11.
p52	'Carver organises for...' Richard van Emden, The Trench, p12.
p53	'W H Carver leaves...' Richard van Emden, The Trench, p14.
p55	'With enough recruits...' Richard van Emden, The Trench, p15.
p57	'With nearly 1000...' Richard van Emden, The Trench, p18.
p64	'Lieutenant Colonel Richardson...' Richard van Emden, The Trench, p29.
p73	'The four Hull Pals...' Richard van Emden, The Trench, p30.
p102	'Uniforms and leather...' Richard van Emden, The Trench, p31.
p104	'Finding it difficult...' Andrews, Canon's Folly, p51.
p105	'During my first...' Andrews, Canon's Folly, p52.
p106	'An invasion scare...' Richard van Emden, The Trench, p30.
p107	'Great excitement when...' Richard van Emden, The Trench, p31.

1915

p111	'By the New...' Richard van Emden, The Trench, p31.
p115	'On arrival in...' Andrews, Canon's Folly, p54.
p122	'We were anchored...' Andrews, Canon's Folly, p55.
p123	'We scrambled into...' Andrews, Canon's Folly, p56.
p129	'By the end...' Andrews, Canon's Folly, p57.
p131	'The endless days...' Andrews, Canon's Folly, p58.
p132	'In the June...' Richard van Emden, The Trench, p32.

p133	'Ration shortages also...' Andrews, Canon's Folly, p59 – 61.
p140	'By the middle...' Andrews, Canon's Folly, p62.
p143	'I hadn't been...' Andrews, Canon's Folly, p63.
p150	'Eventually a ship...' Andrews, Canon's Folly, p66.
p158	'In early November...' Richard van Emden, The Trench, p33.
p163	'By this time...' Andrews, Canon's Folly, p73.

1916

p169	'It was decided...' Andrews, Canon's Folly, p75.
p174	'Not long after...' Andrews, Canon's Folly, p79.
p189	'Sir, I want...' Loss of HMS Russell, Court Martial 1916 The National Archives, Public Records Office, ADM1/8455/97.

1917

p235	'I had been...' Andrews, Canon's Folly, p80.
p241	'Just before I...' Andrews, Canon's Folly, p90.

1918

p276	'In the month...' Andrews, Canon's Folly, p97.
p282	'Of my wounds...' St John, A Tale of Two Rivers.